Do Nothing &
Do Everything

Do Nothing &
Do Everything

An Illustrated New Taoism

Written and Illustrated by

Qiguang Zhao

PARAGON HOUSE
St. Paul, Minnesota

Published in the United States by
Paragon House
St. Paul, Minnesota

Paperback ISBN: 978-1-55778-946-4
E-book ISBN: 978-1-61083-048-5

Library of Congress Cataloging-in-Publication Data

    Zhao, Qiguang, 1948-
    Do nothing and do everything : an illustrated new Taoism /
written and illustrated by Qiguang Zhao. -- 1st ed.
       p. cm.
    Includes bibliographical references and index.
    Summary: "This introduction to ancient Taoism utilizes stories
and illustrations to convey the subtle ideas that go beyond language
as the author applies the Taoist Wu Wei (do nothing) and Wu Bu
Wei (do everything) to modern life"--Provided by publisher.
    ISBN 978-1-55778-889-4 (hardcover : alk. paper)
    1. Taoism. I. Title. II. Title: Illustrated new Taoism.
    BL1920.Z452 2010
    299.5'14--dc22
                         2009038970

Manufactured in the United States of America

The paper used in this publication meets the minimum requirements of American National Standard for Information Sciences—Permanence of Paper for
Printed Library Materials, ANSIZ39.48-1984.

10 9 8 7 6 5 4 3 2 1

Table of Contents

Appendices

to Litao

The stars of wisdom shine over us.
The winds of humor dance between us.
The seas of knowledge carry us to the land of miracle.

Acknowledgements

I would like to express my gratitude to my family for their loving support. I thank my parents for teaching me culture, literature, and life philosophy through a scientific approach. With a wise sense of humor, my father, Professor of Physics Zhao Jingyuan, gives me a love of Chinese tradition and its application to modern life. Also a professor of physics, my mother, Wang Shuxian, loved and wrote Chinese classical poems. We had discussed some of the ideas and illustrations in the book a few months before she passed away. My deepest thanks go to my other family members, especially Zhiming, who edited some of my writings and provided numerous technical supports, Qizheng, who encourages me to present my ideas to a broad audience, and Qida, from whom I learned drawing pictures while telling stories.

I thank Carleton College for the financial and academic support for the project. Beautiful lakes and forests on campus, together with thought-provoking faculty, staff, and students, provide a most serene environment for talking, writing, and thinking. I greatly appreciate my students' support and involvement. Through the years, students in my course "Taoist

Way of Health and Longevity: Tai Chi and Other Forms"
spoke intelligently in crowded classrooms and performed Tai
Chi on campus islands. Sophie Kerman organized primary
materials. Jessica Taylor edited the writing and scanned the
illustrations. Kaitlin Justin, Jane Caffrey, and Zheng Zhu
enthusiastically helped me to complete the final manuscript
and gave me wise input.

Dr. Andrew Weis was enthusiastic about my manuscript
and shared ideas on Taoism with me. He carefully read
through the manuscript and gave me valuable comments and
suggestions. My thanks extend to Mr. Roger Lasley, who read
my manuscript and gave me helpful advice. I am deeply grateful to my colleague Professor Hong Zeng, who offered consistent support.

Many of the opinions in this book were formed when I was
featured on a talk show series about Lao Tzu, aired on Shanghai Television in 2007. I thank Professor Qian Wenzhong of
Fudan University for recommending me for the series. Pro-
ducer Yu Yongjin, anchorman Jin Bo, and director Xia Ning
of Shanghi Television made the show come to life for an audience of millions.

It is impossible to mention all of the people who have
helped and inspired me. To all of them, I give my sincere
thanks.

Preface

When I was completing this book, my mother passed away. She was a professor of physics, a poet, an athlete, and a great mother. Suddenly life and death stand in front of me not as a theoretical discussion in the classroom but as a challenge to reality. It is so difficult for us to accept the deal that life offers us. It seems unfair and crazy. We are given life, and then life is taken away without our agreement. Without a wise mother to protect me, I feel I have an immediate call to figure out the puzzle of life and death.

We do not get to choose when we are going to die or how to die. Yet we can decide when we are going to live. The time is *now*. Seize today and trust not in tomorrow. Eternity does not begin after death, it extends to all of the time in our lives. We are in it now. We can have it if we give up—give up our imagined ability to control life. The moon shines over snow; a planet swings around a star; a black hole devours a constellation. We cannot affect these big phenomena, and we let them be. Our daily life is part of the universe, as every small drop of ocean water reflects the enormous sun. If we cannot change the orbit of the sun, we cannot decide everything in our life either. Therefore, we should accept the pain, treasure the joy, and appreciate life now.

Nowadays, people do not live fully, and they get only about 20 percent out of their lives. This hard-to-get 20 percent of life follows the accepted standards of success and failure. The other 80 percent can be reached effortlessly. Just follow the course of nature, and life will reward you generously. Between your house and your shop, there are numerous little spots of happiness: a squirrel running away from you, a raindrop falling on you, and a stranger greeting you. Just acknowledge them. They always come to you. You do nothing, and nothing is left undone.

A life of reaction is a life of bondage. I believe that one must strive for a life of nonaction or action, not one of reaction. Doing nothing leads to courageous liberation. We should act effortlessly, without anxiety and hesitation. Sitting on the beach quietly is doing nothing. Swimming in the ocean bravely is doing everything. There are no forbidden walls between doing nothing and doing everything. We are free, as long as we cross between the two without anxiety or hesitation.

Do not hesitate when crossing. Do not be bothered by the opinions of others. Hear the call of nature, and act for yourself. You do not want to come to the last moment of your life and find that you have simply lived life's length. You should also have lived the life's width. So when you leave the world, you will not say, "I didn't do this" or "I did that wrong." You are going to say, "I regret nothing. I came. I did nothing. I did it all. As a happy guest, I leave now."

Introduction

This book is based on a course I have taught since 1997, "The Taoist Way of Health and Longevity: Tai Chi and Other Forms." It started out with only six students; by 2006, it had grown to about 60. The class has become one of the most popular courses at Carleton College. In this class, the students and I get lost in the mysterious and serene atmosphere of Taoism. With Lao Tzu, we ride green bulls through Hangu Pass; with Zhuangzi, we watch the fish from the bank of a river; with Liezi, we ride on the wind; with Zhang Sanfeng, we perform Tai Chi by the Cannon River. We promise to meet again in 200 years at the legendary mountain, Dahuang Shan.

On the islands in the campus's two lakes, the students and I get along well. The generational and cultural gaps disappear before the ancient philosophical giants. We even use the first paragraph of the *Tao Te Ching* as our class password. The first student says, "The Tao that can be said..." The second student answers, "...is not the eternal Tao." The first student says, "The name that can be named..." The second student says, "...is not the eternal Name." When they meet again in two hundred years, they may not recognize each other, but they will know each other by this password.

Could you tell us where to find the Tao?

One year, on the last day of our class, some students jumped into the lake and performed Tai Chi to show their Taoist love of water. I realized that American students can really appreciate Taoism, even though their textbook was written in English. This gave me confidence in the cross-linguistic and cross-cultural power of Taoist thought. Thought does not belong only to its birthplace; it belongs to anyone who studies and understands it. Anyone can drink from the source and gain inspiration, health, and longevity.

About the spelling of the Chinese terms: I use the old system for important names and words like *Taoism, Lao Tzu, Confucius*, and *Tai Chi*, because they have become part of the English language. I have moved to the modern pinyin system for less familiar names and words, such as *Zhuangzi, Liezi*, and *Xiang Yu*. The mixture of the old and the new romanization systems reflects the rapid cultural changes that have taken place in China during the past 50 years.

Unless otherwise noted, all quotations from Lao Tzu are from: *The Tao Te Ching: A New Translation and Commentary*, Ellen M. Chen (St. Paul: Paragon House, 1989).

Let's get another perspective on things.

A Manifesto of Modern Taoism

Students: Are you a Taoist?

Qiguang Zhao: I refuse to be named. Ancient Taoist thinkers and their works are ancient history. I am influenced by Taoism, but I keep my spiritual freedom and my right to fly without confines.

Students: What is Applied New Taoism?

Qiguang Zhao: Applied New Taoism seeks to discover the spiritual state between sleeping and waking; between life and death; between present, past, and future; and between Wu Wei and Wu Bu Wei.

Wu Wei, doing nothing, and Wu Bu Wei, doing everything, are our answers to the challenges of modern life. We question the existence and importance of time. *Wu* means "no" and *Wei* means "action," so *Wu Wei* can be translated as "nonaction" or "do nothing." For Wu Bu Wei, the translation is "do everything," because *Bu* means "not," and its combination with *Wu* creates a smart double negative. Thus, *Wu* and *Bu* cancel each other, and *Wu Bu Wei* can be simplified to *Wei* only, with an emphasis on doing all things or leaving nothing undone.

Wu Wei, "do nothing" or "doing nothing," is to follow the course of nature. It is confidence in the universe. Since everything happens within the universe, if you follow the wonder of nature, wonders will occur around you every day.

Wu Wei is wisdom. You tell life, "I trust you; do whatever you want." Life will always reward you with everything surprising. Wu Wei is habit.

Wu Bu Wei, "doing everything," is the creativity to build a good habit. We do not have to solve every basic question of life. We just follow the established good habit, as a mathematician follows established equations without having to prove it every time.

Wu Wei is modesty, knowing that each person has his or her own ambition, each thing has its own owner, and nature and society have their own rules. Wu Bu Wei is courage to navigate through the rules.

Wu Wei is a delight in knowing that everything will be all right. It is not refusing to do anything, it is refusing to do insignificant things. Wu Wei is efficiency. It is the precondition of Wu Bu Wei. Wu Wei requires giving up secondary matters and aiming for the key matters. You can only Wu Bu Wei because you Wu Wei.

Wu Wei is the secret of health. Only if you abandon anxiety can you do anything with a healthy mind and body.

We respect but do not totally agree with ideologies. We do not agree with anyone's opinions: we have opinions of our own.

We gaze at the stars and compare them with ourselves. We do not gloat at our neighbors, envy their successes, or become angry at our differences.

We are alone. We shut the world out as we think, feel, and move. We talk to the world, we listen, we observe, we join, but

The modern meets the ancient.

we keep Tao at the core, like a cliff hanging above the surging ocean. Let the world make ripples, waves, or storms on the ocean; our cliff stays high and grows higher.

We think with our bodies. Usually, the body is directed by the mind. Yet when we move with uniform motion, our bodies give us a message, a biofeedback, which brings the mind closer to the uniform motion of the universe.

We create a surreal world. We fly in the clouds, we ride rainbows.

The world has waited too long for a voice with fresh ideas and new approaches to life. We hope to create such a voice by echoing an old tune, a voice that soothes the heart and strengthens the mind in a new established form. We want to create a mode of communication between humans that is beyond language.

We are not scholars who make every effort to understand books. We are artists who apply our knowledge to our lives. I invite you to creation, a forging of the missing links between ancient worlds and our life. Let us go through the thorns of elite scholarship, through the bushes of vulgar devices, and visit a quiet, forgotten land.

Let us find love, in a broad sense, a love whose object is not one person called *Lover*, not a group of persons called *Class* or *Nation*, but rather a concept of ultimate beauty that extends to the ends of the universe. I want to inform you, coach you, inspire you, and then ask you to meet the challenges of the world, to form healthy, balanced ways of thinking, living, approaching, and existing.

We know how to relax and do nothing, or Wu Wei, because without doing anything, the stars twinkle quietly numerous light-years from earth, and the earth rotates on its axis once every 24 hours. If the universe can, so can we; we know how to do everything without worrying, because we only belong to this world for a short while.

2 Many Thinkers, One Tao

In a culture dominated by Confucianism (which represents, among other things, the moralistic, the official, and the respectable), these lonely thinkers echo each other with an individualistic, unconventional, and spontaneous voice.

Lao Tzu was the author of the *Tao Te Ching* and an older contemporary of Confucius in the Spring and Autumn period (722–481 BCE). He was born in Zhou State and was the librarian of the Zhou Emperor. We are not certain whether he was one person or many; it is possible that a number of people wrote the *Tao Te Ching*. However, as with Shakespeare, the exact identity of the author is less important than the content of the works. According to legend, Lao Tzu was born with gray hair and left China riding backwards on an ox; at the gate of China, the gatekeeper persuaded him to write the Tao Te Ching as a last record of his philosophy.

Zhuangzi lived in the fourth century BCE. He was a rival of Confucianism and a follower of Lao Tzu, and in his writings, he often satirized the popular Confucianist and Mohist philosophies of the time. Together, Lao Tzu and Zhuangzi are considered the fathers of Taoist philosophy (as distinguished from Taoist religion).

Liezi was another representative Taoist. The teachings of Liezi were close to those of Zhuangzi. He was supposed to have lived during the early part of the Warring States Period (476–221 BCE). However, the extant version of his works reflects the thinking and writing style of later scholars.

Confucius (551–479 BCE) has been the dominant Chinese philosopher both morally and politically. In the Warring States Period, Mencius (c.390–305 BCE) extended and systematized Confucius's ideas. With the Han Dynasty's (206 BCE–220 CE) adoption of Confucianism as the official moral and political doctrine of the State, the Confucian tradition became so broad that "scholar" became all but synonymous with "Confucian." Confucius discusses the Tao quite often, but his Tao is entirely different from that of Lao Tzu and Zhuangzi. He is in many ways a rival, in opposition to Taoism, though he had a great respect for Lao Tzu and his ideas. The six main Confucian principles are loyalty, filial piety, ritual, righteousness, honesty, and shame. The Confucian emphasis on ritual and obligation is in strong contrast to Taoist philosophy.

Confucius asked in the *Analects*:

> Is it not a great pleasure to study and to practice what you
> have learned?
> Is it not a happiness to have friends coming from far away?
> Is he not a gentleman who is not bothered by people who
> do not recognize him?[1]

Compare this with Lao Tzu's three questions after he suggested "Abandon learning and put an end to your troubles":

Is there a difference between yes and no?
Is there a difference between good and evil?
Is it not nonsense that I must fear what others fear?

There were 200 years between Lao Tzu and Zhuangzi; there are over 2000 years between Zhuangzi and us.

Here, we gather to answer Zhuangzi as he answered Lao Tzu.

If we cannot, who can?
If we won't, who will?
We heard your voice, 2000 years ago.
We saw your banners, 15,000 miles away.

Together, we go rambling without a destination. We even things out. We find what matters in life.

I learned the following comical poem from my father, who often recited it during the Cultural Revolution. It is a few lines from a Peking opera, recited by a robber who, sword in hand, stops the traveling hero and roars:

> I opened this road
> I planted this tree
> You want to go ahead
> Leave money to me
> It will be too bad
> If you do not agree
> I will chop your head
> You cannot flee

The hero just mocks the robber and announces, "I would give you my money, but I have two friends who do not agree."

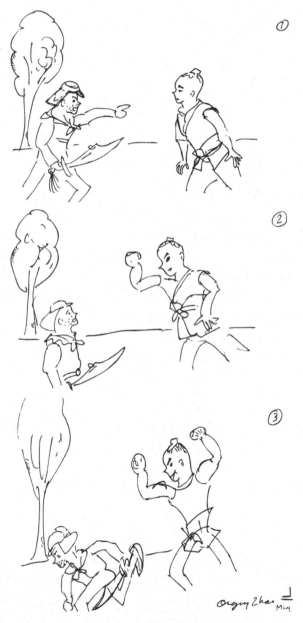

"Which two friends?" the robber demands.

The hero raises his right fist. "This is the first friend of mine." He raises his left. "This is my second friend."

"Ah ya-ya!" The robber yells as he jumps on the hero. They fight fiercely, and the hero eventually wins.

We can have two friends in our lives: Confucius and Lao Tzu. Following just one would leave us incomplete. We can be practical and spiritual, awake and dreaming. With a balance between direction and nondirection, between action and inaction, we will follow a middle path.

3 Take It Easy and Take Care

Confucianism and Taoism can be seen as two opposite responses to social pressures. While Confucianism is concerned with social relations and conduct, Taoism has a much more individualistic and carefree character and is greatly influenced by nature.

Two American expressions reflect these opposite attitudes. Both expressions mean "goodbye" but can be seen as standing for Confucian and Taoist life philosophies. When I first came to the United States for graduate school in the early 1980s, I found that Americans say goodbye differently than what I learned in my textbooks in China. In those days, students learned only formal British English in China. There were several ways to say goodbye, even including "Cheerio" or "Farewell until we meet again."

When I finished my first class in an American classroom, I walked up to the professor and tested my textbook sentence: "Farewell until we meet again," I said. He answered with a smile, "Take it easy." I took the expression literally, as advice, thinking I must look too nervous in class. So I tried to loosen up a bit in the next class meeting and even ventured to chime in with my opinions. At the end of the next class, I walked up to him again and bade him adieu. "Take care," he advised. Instead of urging me to take it easy, he warned me to "take care!" I thought I was being admonished for my carelessness, thought I might have been relaxed to a fault. Indeed, I should take care of my performance.

After several cycles of taking it easy and taking care, I realized that Americans just say to "take care" or "take it easy" as a casual way of saying goodbye, without meaning to give advice or warning. Now when I hear people say to "take care" or "take it easy," I cannot help smiling, because the casual parting expressions remind me of when I first came to the United States.

These expressions also reflect the opposed attitudes of Confucius and Lao Tzu. A Confucian would say, "Take care" and a Taoist would say, "Take it easy."

Lao Tzu counseled people to turn away from the endless river of human care and return to their natural wellspring. According to Confucius, the process of learning the names used in the classics helped one to make distinctions between good and evil, beautiful and ugly, high and low, "being" and "nonbeing." According to Lao Tzu, to abandon knowledge is to abandon names, distinctions, tastes, and desires. This would result in nonaction, doing nothing, or spontaneous behavior (Wu Wei) and lead us to spiritual freedom.

When they face the world, Confucians take care, while Taoists take it easy. Confucians worry about future consequences, while Taoists enjoy the present harmony. Confucians hold life and names dear. They climb on the mountain of life and see that the path to glory is always rugged. They counsel caution and warn fellow climbers, "Take care."

Taoists know that life comes and goes. They deny none of their natural penchants, repress none of their desires, and never feel the spur of reputation. They saunter through life, gathering its pleasures as the whim moves them. Since they shun personal fame and gains, they are beyond care and fear. Name and gain are temporary visitors, not permanent residents of the world. They climb the mountain of life, see the setting sun gild the sky, and announce triumphantly: "Take it easy."

Take it easy and enjoy the scenery. Take care and do not tip the boat.

4 Take It Easy, but Take It

A Confucian Taoist would say "Take it easy, but take it." If you cannot take care as a Confucian, and will not take it easy as a Taoist, you can take it easy, but take it. This is probably closest to our concept of Wu Wei and Wu Bu Wei. Wu Wei is not passively doing nothing, but rather doing everything effortlessly, as bamboo shadows sweep the terrace without stirring any dust, as moonlight pierces a marsh but leaves no traces. There is a Chinese idiom, "Push the boat with the current," meaning to use an opportunity to go forward, or to give judicious guidance according to circumstances.

Push the boat with the current.

15

Ronald Reagan was the only American president to quote Lao Tzu in a state of the union address: "Govern a great nation as you would cook a small fish," he said. That is, when you cook a small fish, you should not flip it too much or overdo it. He was promoting the conservative ideology of the free market as an engine of economic progress, but he also revealed this basic idea in his approach to world affairs.

Some people credit Reagan for destroying the Soviet Union. His voice, with his actor's rhythmic tone, still echoes today: "Mr. Gorbachev, tear down that wall!" Lo, the Berlin Wall fell in no time: the Iron Curtain fell, and America became the only superpower. The whole Western world stood up and roared, "Well done, Big Ronny!" Who is this Ronny guy? A magician? A Solomon? A First Emperor of the Qin Dynasty? What magic did he perform to change the color of the "Evil Empire"? What wisdom won him such loving respect? What power did he possess to destroy the supposedly invincible adversary?

His cheerleaders could not rationalize the sudden fall of the "Evil Empire," nor could they figure out how Reagan contributed to it. So they surmised that Reagan lured the Soviet Union into an arms race, which dragged the Soviet economy down. While Reagan took afternoons off for golf on weekdays, the Empire spanning six time zones worked itself to death. As a matter of fact, the arms race between the Soviet Union and the United States had already been going on for 70 years before Reagan and Gorbachev, and every American president had tried to beat the Soviet Union in that race. Nobody needs to lure anybody to do something both have already been doing wholeheartedly for 70 years.

The Soviet Union collapsed under its own weight. President Reagan's magic, his wisdom, and his power were Wu Wei, or doing nothing. Reagan did nothing to destroy the Soviet Union. He just left the fish alone and let it cook itself. The Soviet Union fell because of its own internal faults.

When we say he did nothing, we are not discrediting him. Quite the contrary, America should be grateful to this president. If he had done something, such as invade that country, the Soviet Union would have lasted a few more decades at least. Both Napoleon and Hitler found that they could not defeat Russia by invading it; in fact, their attacks only made it stronger. The power of American presidents is limited domestically because of the constitutional division of powers, but as commanders in chief, presidents are almost unlimited decision makers in international affairs. If they want to leave a presidential legacy, or if they want to test the clout of the military, aggressiveness can be very attractive. The tragedy of the leaders of the great powers is that they do not know how to stand and do nothing.

We are often put in an unfavorable condition or circumstance. However, unfavorable circumstances can also give us opportunities. In addition, the world is more complex than we understand, and we do not really know what a situation means for us. When we are unsure, the best strategy is to accept the situation and go with the flow. Lao Tzu said, "Misfortune is the root of good fortune; good fortune gives birth to misfortune." When an unfavorable situation arises, we must first

Wu Wei: accept and understand its possible potential, and gracefully turn the tables. If it works, we are happy. If it does not work, we at least have avoided doubling our misfortune by going in a wrong direction.

5 Wu Wei

Wu Wei is a basic principle of Taoism. *Wu* can be translated as "no"; *Wei* can be translated as "do" or "accomplish." The literal meaning of *Wu Wei* is "nonaction" or "without action." Why Wu Wei? And if we are not to do anything, what should we do?

Wu Wei means to follow the course of nature. It means to break the chain of worries and realize that not everything leads to your goal in life; it means to give yourself a break realizing that the process is more beautiful than the goal.

Nonaction is building a habit. That habit leads your life. You cannot make a decision every day or every minute. Should I get up now or at 7:30 AM? Should I smoke or not? Should I be an optimist or a worrier? When a habit is built, you are liberated from hourly, daily, weekly, or yearly action. You do not have to solve every problem from the very beginning. You do not have to agonize over the question of whether to be or not to be, because "to be" is already a habit. We should have seven, seventy, seven hundred, and seven million good habits, but we do not have to rebuild them or rationalize them every time. With good habits, we are free from making "much ado about nothing." A sparrow flies in the azure sky, seemingly without effort. Hundreds of muscles are working, but the sparrow does not have to think about each one. It simply has a good habit, a habit so natural and serene that it is effortless, like bamboo that grows by a stream, the boat that floats on a river, and the clouds that slide on the sky.

A good habit, like a boat anchored in a quiet harbor after a storm, is established by doing nothing after a lot of doing everything.

Wu Wei is frequently misunderstood. In modern China, if you tell a person you follow Taoism, sometimes you will receive a comment like, "Oh, is it the philosophy of Wu Wei? Why do you follow the philosophy of idleness?" As a matter of fact, Wu Wei is not passively doing nothing, but rather knowing when to act and when not to act. It is often included in the paradox Wei Wu Wei, or acting nonaction. The goal of Wu Wei is to achieve a state of spontaneous alignment with the Tao, and, as a result, obtain a perfect form of supple and invisible power.

The Sage is occupied with acts without effort, messages without speaking, and successes without exertion. Lao Tzu teaches without wordiness, produces without possessing, and creates without regard for result. Not overdoing things and doing them at the proper time is the key to success. Taoism recognizes that the universe works harmoniously in its own ways; as humans put forth their will against the world they interrupt the existing harmony. This is not to say that we ought not to exert our will to act. Rather it is knowing whether, when, and how to act in relation to natural processes.

Wu Wei has also been interpreted as the art of letting be, or creative quietude. This does not mean a laziness of action or a dullness of the mind; rather it is an alert and effortless determination to obey the rules of the Way. One way of thinking of Wu Wei is through Lao Tzu's words about how to govern a big nation. The advice is to govern a big nation as you would fry a small fish: too much flipping and the fish is ruined.

Lao Tzu said:

> To pursue learning one increases daily.
> To pursue Tao one decreases daily.
> To decrease and again to decrease
> Until one arrives at not doing.
> Not doing and yet nothing is not done.
> Always take the empire when there are no businesses.
> If there are businesses,
> It is not worthwhile to take the empire.
> (Chen: *The Tao Te Ching*, Chapter 48)

In learning, we always pick up more. In Taoism, we drop things. Since our infancy, we have learned many things that separate us from the universe. We worry about trivial matters, like wealth and prestige. Now we want to return to our origins, to be more like a baby and forget these distractions. We want to do nothing. This is Wu Wei.

By choosing nonaction, we choose to empty ourselves and go with the flow rather than fight the current. Nonaction does not mean not doing, stopping the natural progression of events; instead, nonaction means to follow nature's course without fighting, striving, or resisting change. We are like water, like the empty vessel, formless and nameless; and in so being, we cannot act: we must accept what challenges the universe throws at us. At the same time, by fulfilling our purpose and allowing ourselves to be empty, we are doing all that we need to do. We do nothing and, in so doing, accomplish everything.

Wu Wei is an act of spontaneity and effortlessness. Zhuangzi refers to this type of existence as *xiao yao,* or "purposeless wandering." It should not be considered laziness or mere passivity. Instead, it is the practice of going with nature, or swimming with the current. The Chinese expression *"ting qi zi ran,"* "let nature take its course," and the English axiom "Go with the flow" are close approximations of this fundamental Taoist principle.

Perhaps the most glorious and prosperous period in China was the Rule of Wen and Jing (180 BCE–141 BCE) of the Han Dynasty, known for the benevolence and thriftiness of the rulers. These two emperors reduced taxes and other burdens on the people, practiced pacifism, and preserved general political stability. The Rule of Wen and Jing was marked by Taoist influence on its political theory due to the influence of Empress Dou, who was the wife of Emperor Wen and mother to Emperor Jing. Unfortunately, when she died during the reign of her grandson, Emperor Wu, the Taoist leadership came to an end. The Rule of Wen and Jing was exceptional and is viewed as the Golden Age of Chinese history. The country was so rich that the coins in the treasury piled up into mountains. The strings that held them together rotted and broke, and many coins fell out of the building, along with piles of extra grain from the government granaries. Almost no emperors in Chinese history have reached as high a level of peace and prosperity as these two emperors and their strong Wu Wei wife and mother.

The problem with other emperors is that they did too much. Take, for example, the First Emperor of the Qin Dynasty (221 BCE–206 BCE). He could not stop after he unified China and went on to undertake some Herculean construction projects, including building the Great Wall. He built an enormous mausoleum for himself, including an underground terra cotta army of 8,000 soldiers. He burned almost all existing books and buried 460 scholars alive. He could not be satisfied with doing nothing. But public works and attacks on those who opposed him were too great of a burden for the population. Qin rule, supposedly the strongest in Chinese history, came to an end shortly after his death. It lasted only 15 years. The Qin emperor's problem was that he was not able to do nothing. When his power and desire combined, ferocious fire burned his dynasty to ashes. I am not saying that he should have been dormant in his throne, but he should have known where to stop.

Fortunately and unfortunately, most of us do not have the power of emperors. However, we can become Wu Wei emperors of our own territory. Let us spend one day as free as water, as nature, and not be thrown off track by every petty noise of the world. We can rise early, gently, and not be upset by the terrible rapids and whirlpools we encounter. Let us sit quietly by the window, watch the clouds float over the horizon, watch the leaves fall, the flowers bloom, and the seasons come and go. Then we can say we have brought peace to our reign. Our land is small, and our power is limited; but with our limited power to rule our limited territory, we can create a place. Peace is the first form of serenity and happiness. If everyone has found peace within, there will be peace everywhere.

In this world, life is eating everyone up. People are pressed to act, sometimes irrationally. Let us set aside a serenity into which the world cannot intrude. There is an ancient Wu Wei that we carry in our hearts. Sometimes we are trapped in a corner and forced to make decisions. We often assume that if we do not decide, our little world will fall apart. As a matter of fact, the two decisions may be both right and wrong. We only find out what was right after the decision is made and the consequences have unfolded. So it is better not to worry, but to be at peace.

Lao Tzu sometimes puts the verb *Wei* (to act or practice) before *Wu Wei* (no action). He said:

Do when there is nothing to do,
Manage affairs when there are none to manage,
Know by not knowing.
Regard the great as small, the much as little.
Repay injury with *te*.
Plan the difficult while it is easy.
Accomplish the great when it is small.
(Chen, *The Tao Te Ching*, Chapter 63)

Doing nothing is hard work. Keeping the status quo is as difficult as creating change. Being still requires effort. This is true for anything, from humans to stars.

If each person has peace in his or her heart,
there will be peace in the world.

When a star gets sufficiently dense, the repulsion caused by the Exclusion Principle would be less than the attraction of gravity. The Nobel laureate astrophysicist Chandrasekhar calculated that a cold star of more than about one and a half times the mass of the sun would not be able to support itself against its own gravity. This mass is now known as the *Chandrasekhar limit*.[2]

Maintaining our present position is a hard job. Just as the star supports itself against its own gravity, Lao Tzu said "Wei Wu Wei," or "act nonaction." So nonaction is an action: just as a star maintains its own gravity, a human attains longevity and humankind protects the environment. Many people cannot support themselves; they destroy themselves with gambling, drugs, and smoking. Maintaining a healthy life is both Wu Wei and Wu Bu Wei. Not having a bad habit takes as much work as having a good habit.

NOTES

1. Stephen Hawking, *The Theory of Everything* (Beverly Hills: New Millennium Press, 2002), 50.

6 Wu Bu Wei

Taoism is not a passive philosophy; it advocates adventures, as long as you enjoy the adventure for itself and do not focus on the aim.

> Tao everlasting does not act,
> And yet nothing is not done.
> If kings and barons can abide by it,
> The ten thousand things will transform by themselves.
> If in transforming desire is aroused,
> I shall suppress it by the nameless uncarved wood.
> With the nameless uncarved wood,
> There shall be no desire.
> Without desire there is thus quietude.
> The world shall be self-ordered.
> (Chen, *The Tao Te Ching*, Chapter 37)

In the pursuit of learning, every day something is acquired.

> To pursue Tao one decreases daily.
> To decrease and again to decrease,
> Until one arrives at not doing.
> Not doing and yet nothing is not done.
> Always take the empire when there are no businesses.
> If there are no businesses,
> It is not worthwhile to take the empire.
> (Chen, *The Tao Te Ching*, Chapter 48)

Remember when we discussed Lao Tzu's Chapter 48 in the context of Wu Wei, doing nothing? The story is a little more complicated than that.

In both Chapter 37 and Chapter 48, Lao Tzu twice uses the words *Wu Wei* (literally, "no do" or "doing nothing") and *Wu Bu Wei* ("no no do," or "not doing nothing," or "doing everything"). *Wu Bu Wei* is traditionally translated as "nothing is left undone." *Wu Bu Wei* is a consequence clause, an upshot of Wu Wei, as if Lao Tzu is saying, "If you do nothing, then everything will be done."

However, in the original Chinese, Lao Tzu uses the conjunction *er* between Wu Wei and Wu Bu Wei. *Er* most closely translates to "but" or "and," not "therefore." Wu Wei and

When you play chess, you can do nothing on a cliff and
do everything while you are flying.

Wu Bu Wei are parallel clauses, not expressions of cause and effect.

Lao Tzu thunders the most important message to us from 2,500 years ago: Do nothing and do everything. Not only does this change the meaning of our philosophy, it changes our roles in life. We are not passive objects, waiting for everything to "be done" through our nonaction; rather we are the subjects of our own lives. We use both Wu Wei and Wu Bu Wei; we do nothing and do everything.

The Tao abides in nonaction *and* in action: we do everything by doing nothing. Since man follows Tao and Tao follows nature, we should do nothing against nature. To understand Wu Bu Wei, think of the Uncertainty Principle of physics. According to Stephen Hawking:

> The uncertainty principle implies that the more accurately one knows one of these qualities, the less accurately one can know the other. So in empty space the field cannot be fixed at exactly zero, because then it would have both a precise value, zero, and a precise rate of change, also zero. Instead, there must be a certain minimum amount of uncertainty, or quantum fluctuations, in the value of a field.[3]

Therefore, absolute Wu, absolute negation, is impossible. There must be something in the Wu; you must have something to negate. Absolute Wu Wei is also impossible, because one cannot make absolutely zero change. In the "field" of action and nonaction, the demarcation line between Wu Wei and Wu Bu Wei is uncertain. We travel between Wu Wei and Wu Bu Wei, usefulness and uselessness.

Our key figure for Doing Nothing and Doing Everything.

Here is a story told by Zhuangzi:

Zhuangzi was walking in the mountains and saw a huge tree lush with leaves. All the woodcutters left it alone. Zhuangzi asked a woodcutter why. The woodcutter answered, "That tree is useless." Zhuangzi commented, "This tree is useless and can live out its life."

Zhuangzi left the mountain and went to stay at a friend's house. The friend was very pleased to see him and asked a boy to kill a goose in Zhuangzi's honor. The boy said, "One goose can honk and the other cannot. Which one should I kill?" The friend said, "Kill the one that cannot honk."

The next day, a student asked Zhuangzi, "The other day, we saw a tree that could live out its life because it was useless. Just now, we saw a goose killed because it was useless. What do you choose, master? Usefulness or uselessness?"

Zhuangzi smiled. "I will stay between usefulness and uselessness. This position looks useful but is useless, and we cannot avoid the burden. It is different to drift with the Tao; there is neither praise nor blame. Sometimes you're a dragon, sometimes you're a snake, floating with time, never focusing on one thing, up and down, using harmony as measurement. Swimming with the ancestor of the ten thousand things, taking things as things, not being taken as a thing, how can you be burdened?"[4]

We have spoken about nonaction: staying weak, staying low. On the other hand, when the time comes, do not hesitate to go high—just so long as you know that it is temporary. In your life, you can be successful or unsuccessful: it doesn't matter, as long as you flow with the time. Your purpose will be the realization that you are part of the universe.

When a triumphant general returned to Rome, he would ride through the street, and the crowd cheered on both sides. Yet he always had a slave sitting in the carriage, to whisper in his ear: *"Respice post te! Hominem te esse memento! Memento mori!"* ("Look behind you! Remember you are only a man! Remember you will die!") The general would smile.

According to the Uncertainty Principle, there is much in life that we cannot control. Since we cannot control the universe, we do nothing. Since we cannot control the universe, we can also do everything, just for the fun of it. The earth moves, but we do not feel its motion. We do nothing, but we do it all.

Our temple is supported by separate pillars: Wu Wei and Wu Bu Wei. We cannot say that today our temple will lean on only one of them. We cannot say, "Today I do nothing; tomorrow I will do everything." We live in the vague domain between doing everything and doing nothing. We shift between Wu Wei and Wu Bu Wei, just as modern binary systems shift between 0 and 1. Making ourselves artificial obstacles to the transition between doing nothing and doing everything causes mental pain and operates against the Uncertainty Principle.

Cause and effect are not as they seem. We can do nothing, we can do everything: the result is the same. In time, everything in the universe will end. Even when we achieve our goals, we cannot own them, and they may not turn out as we had planned. Our expectations may betray us, and when all is said and done, all of our actions will be lost in the flow of nature.

NOTES

2. Stephen Hawking, *The Theory of Everything* (Beverly Hills: New Millennium Press, 2002), 82.

3. Stories from *Zhuangzi* are translated by the author, unless otherwise noted.

7 The Universe and Us

The best show in the universe is the universe. Look at the starry sky. What a show!

The best show of the world is the world.

The universe is big, and we are small. When we are small, so are our problems. Let the starry sky lead us to a time that is neither the past nor the future nor the present. Let the stars lead us to a space beyond life and death. The best show in the universe is the universe!

"What a piece of work is a man," Hamlet says. "How noble in reason, how infinite in faculties; in form and movement, how expressive and admirable; in action, how like an angel, in apprehension, how like a god." This is why he is crazy. He thinks human beings are larger than the world, and his problems grow out of his control. The self-centered people will be punished by the world.

Who agrees that humans are so great? Do birds agree? Do ants agree? Do monkeys agree? Even cats do not agree. Only dogs, our sole companions after 15,000 years of domestication, might agree that we are "the beauty of the world, the paragon of animals!" Only dogs look at us and try to understand us as if we were a piece of Shakespeare's poetry. The problem is, if your best friend was the only one to call you "the beauty of the world," it might be wise not to believe him. So I urge you not to watch men only, but to watch, as Hamlet said, "the air, look you, this brave o'erhanging firmament, this majestical roof fretted with golden fire."

Many people ignore the beauty of the world and the splendid show of the universe. Hamlet noticed the beauty of the world and of humanity, but his problems grew so big that he could not draw strength from this. Renaissance humanism, as represented by Hamlet, put humanity at the center of the universe, which during the Middle Ages had been God's place. Humans took up the burden of to do or not to do, or in Hamlet's case, to be or not to be. According to Taoism, everything that bothers us is small compared to the vastness of time and space. When you realize how small you are, you no longer believe you are a god; without that pressure, you can move freely with the universe with no illusions of grandeur.

We cannot claim to be gods, but how much more freedom we have in the knowledge of our insignificance!

We are not the center of the world,
although our best friend may think so.

Zhuangzi told a story to explain our limitations:

The autumn flood came; the Yellow River swelled with water from its hundred tributaries. You could not tell a horse from a cow on the opposite bank. The river god was contented and thought he had swallowed every beautiful thing. He followed the current to the east and reached the North Sea. He looked east and did not see the limit of the water. He looked around and sighed to Ruo, the ocean god. "As the saying goes, 'One who has heard a hundred truths thinks he's the best in the world.' This is me. Now I know you are infinite. If I had not come to your door, I would be in great danger of being loved by all people."

Ruo said, "You cannot tell a frog in a well about the ocean, because it is limited by space. You cannot tell a summer insect about ice, because it is limited by time. You cannot tell a bookish scholar about the Tao, because he is limited by education. Today, you have broken out of your cage and watched the ocean, and you know your own pettiness. Now we can talk about great wisdom."

Like the river god and the frog in the well, our abilities of perception are tiny compared to the vastness of the universe. We are just small creatures, and we are only here for a short visit. Let nature take care of the order of things.

Nature heals our wounds, gives us freedom, and offers us help we cannot give to each other. Zhuangzi told another story:

> When a spring dries up, and the fish are stranded on the land, they keep each other moist with their own bodies and with the foam they spit at each other. They would be better off if they could forget each other in the rivers and lakes. Rather than praising the sage king Yao and denouncing the cruel tyrant Jic, we could forget both of them and let their Ways dissolve.

Although they spit foam at each other during a drought, the fish would rather be able to forget each other in the joy of swimming. We would rather forget the trivial events of our time and lose them in the vastness of the universe. Forget these distinctions, forget these anxieties; they are all small compared to the Tao.

There is a story recorded by a Warring States statesman, Lu Buwei:

A man of Chu State lost a bow but decided he would not look for it. "A Chu man lost it, and a Chu man will find it," he said. "Why bother to look for it?"

Confucius heard this story and commented: "The word 'Chu' can be dropped."

Lao Tzu heard the story and commented, "The word 'man' can be dropped."

(Qiguang Zhao heard the story and commented, "The words 'lost' and 'found' can be dropped.")

The Chu man is patriotic: whether the bow is his or not does not matter to him, as long as it still belongs to a citizen of Chu.

Confucius is a humanitarian: it does not matter what country the bowfinder belongs to, as long as the bow belongs to a human being.

Lao Tzu is a Taoist: it does not matter if the bow belongs to a human being or to a mound of dirt; it belongs to nature. (Lu Buwei said Lao Tzu is the most selfless among the three.)

Qiguang Zhao says the bow is not ours anyway. In the year 2007, astronomers demoted Pluto, but it doesn't matter to Pluto whether or not we call it a planet. The bow is itself; the "lost" and "found" only create an illusion of attachment to things.

楚人失弓，楚人得之

A person of Chu loses it; a person of Chu finds it.

A person loses it; a person finds it. —Confucius

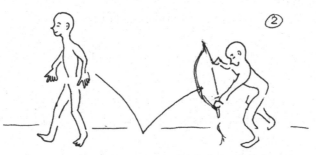

失之，得之

It is lost; It is found. —Lao Tzu

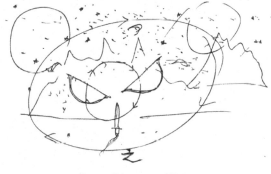

It. —Qiguang Zhao

What does it matter if it is lost or found? It is all part of the universe. As words reduce, our view enlarges.

Reversing

Returning is the movement of Tao.
Weak is the functioning of Tao.
The ten thousand things under heaven are born of being.
Being is born of non-being.
(Chen, *The Tao Te Ching*, Chapter 40)

If it does not work, just try reversing it.

The universe began from a very small point. The density of the primordial universe was so great that millions of tons were concentrated in a point as big as the tip of a needle. It is now expanding, and there are three theories of what its ultimate fate will be. The first is that it will continue to expand forever, spreading all its matter and energy so thin that no life of any kind will survive. The second is that the expansion will continue, but will slow down and eventually stabilize. The third possibility—which is my favorite, because it is the most Taoist—is that once the universe has stopped expanding, it will begin to contract again. It will contract back to the size of a needlepoint. When this happens, gravity will become so strong that everything will stop moving. Wu Wei triumphs in the end. All life, information, and history will be lost; it will return to the great emptiness. Then why shouldn't the Big Bang happen again?

The universe is moving in a cycle, expanding and condensing between two extremes. Because we live in the universe, whatever we do is a part of the universal cycle of reversal. Everything will eventually transform and become its opposite, and we can learn this best from watching the universe.

A student once asked me, "What is the opposite of time?"

Without thinking, I answered "space."

What is time? We think of time as the years, days, hours, and minutes that make up our lives. Superficially, it is also a measurement of movement through space: the sun rises, the sun sets, the earth rotates around the sun. Neither time nor space exists without the other; they are complementary, like the Taoist yin and yang.

Most people agree that the universe is expanding, and many say that at some point, it will begin to shrink. Everything transforms into its opposite: the universe will become smaller and smaller, and then it will shrink to a single point. That is to say someday, everything in the universe will stop. Time and space can become each other, and someday they will both disappear. The law of the unity of opposites is the fundamental law of the universe. Everything is a unity of opposites; everything exists because of its opposite. There is yin because there is yang; there is up because there is down; there is white because there is black; there is male because there is female.

Everything exists because of its opposite, and everything will become its opposite someday. What expands must shrink. The universe, when it stops expanding, will contract into a black hole. The hardest tree, when blown over by a strong wind, will decay and become soft.

Reversing is the motion of the Tao. Turn this book

反者道之用
Reversing is the
motion of the Tao

(Qi Zhu
zhong

upside-down. Just as these drawings show different faces when you look at them upside-down, the world looks different when you look at it in reverse. Try standing on your head: It really changes your perspective on things.

Reversing does not mean that you must change between just two opposites; often, there is a whole new dimension you have to consider. This is what we call "thinking outside the box."

In the following ancient Chinese story a man and his elderly advisor consider different options but get stuck in only two dimensions:

A man from Lu carrying a long pole tried to enter the city gate. First, he held the pole upright, but it was too tall, and he could not get it through the gate. Then he tried holding it

Sometimes the correct solution is the simplest.

horizontally, but the pole was too wide, and it still could not pass through. He was stumped. An old man came along and said, "I am not a sage, but I do have a lot of practical experience. Why not cut the pole in two at the middle?" So the man cut the pole in two at the middle.

The best way to go around a barrier is to go through it.

Benjamin Franklin was certain of two things: death and taxes. Taoists are simpler. We are certain of only one thing: change, in all dimensions. Do not worry that your answer may be too simple. The simple answer usually works better than the complex one.

Lao Tzu was respected for his dialectical understanding of change—everything changes to its extreme, hence the paradox that to achieve a goal, one should begin with its opposite. To be yang, one must retain yin. To have strength, one must retain weakness. Because things develop to their opposite, when they reach the extreme, one should interfere as little as possible with nature. The best sovereign does not exercise active rule. Everything exists because of its opposite, and everything changes towards its opposite. If you have life, you will develop toward death. Because everything moves toward its opposite, if you want to be strong, you need weakness. The wise, the heroic, and the strong must be foolish, cowardly, and weak.

9 Naming

Tao that can be spoken of
Is not the Everlasting Tao.
Name that can be named
Is not the Everlasting name.
Nameless, the origin of heaven and earth;
Named, the mother of ten thousand things.
(Chen, *The Tao Te Ching,* Chapter 1)

Lao Tzu tried to distinguish between the namable and unnamable in the world. The former included the specific things, and the latter included the eternal, limitless, and primitive universe. Thus, the unnamable is the beginning of heaven and earth and the mother of all things. The Tao is unnamable because it is the beginning of all beginnings and never ceases to be. It is all embracing, infinite, and the source of all specific shapes. Words are not enough to define the Tao; it is greater than a single word and cannot be confined to language. Expression goes beyond words. The Tao encompasses the universe; how can the infinite be expressed in a single name?

The first chapter of *The Tao Te Ching*, quoted above, is like a knock on the door. When we open the door to the concept of the nameless, we begin to experience a wider meaning to the universe.

When we refuse to name the Tao, we perform our first act of Wu Wei, or nondoing. We do not fight to confine the Tao within one name or category. In letting the principle of our lives remain nameless, we are embracing the freedom of the Tao, which includes the expanse of the ocean, the boundlessness of the starry sky, and the depth of the human spirit.

Without names, we are undefined; without definition, we have no meaning; without meaning, our borders are limitless. We are not defined by others: we define ourselves. To do that, we need a beginning. We choose to begin nowhere, with the emptiness that came before the modern world gave us names.

10 Emptiness

Tao is a whirling emptiness,
Yet in use is inexhaustible.
Fathomless,
It seems to be the ancestor of
ten thousand beings.
It blunts the sharp,
Unties the entangled,
Harmonizes the bright,
Mixes the dust.
Dark,
It seems perhaps to exist.
I do not know whose child it is,
It is an image of what precedes
God.
(*Tao Te Ching*, Chapter 4)

Thirty spokes share one hub to
make a wheel.
Through its non-being,
There is the use of the carriage.
Mold clay into a vessel.
Through its non-being,
There is the use of the vessel.
Cut out doors and windows to
make a house.
Through its non-being,
There is the use of the house.
Therefore in the being of a
thing,
There lies the benefit.
In the non-being of a thing,
There lies its use.
(*Tao Te Ching*, Chapter 11)

The house exists because of the space inside, not because of the beams and materials. The bowl itself is not useful; the empty space within a bowl is useful. Like the house and the bowl, we are no longer useful if we have no internal space. We find this physical space by exhaling, but we also must empty ourselves of the weight of the world, which we have wrongly placed upon our own shoulders. We must rid ourselves of anxiety, preconceptions, greed, and false ambitions. As humans, and not gods, we have no need for these worries, which we ultimately cannot control. We must become the empty vessel, nameless and receptive to the beauty of nature.

The usefulness of emptiness.

11 | Water

A person with superior goodness is like water,
Water is good in benefiting all beings,
Without contending with any.
Situated in places shunned by many others,
Thereby it is near Tao.
(Chen, *The Tao Te Ching*, Chapter 8)

Water is the essence of Wu Wei, nonaction. As water flows downhill, it takes the path of least resistance and follows the contours of the land. It takes many shapes and adapts itself to the form of its surroundings. Though many may not wish to venture into the low places of the world, there is nothing undignified about water. Though it is humble enough to enter into dark places, the humility and weakness of water is its greatest strength: by not striving, it carves away caves and smoothes the most jagged of rocks. Behave like water, take on its nature: I invite you to swim in the world.

The Chinese dragon flies in the air, but it primarily behaves like a water god. It is believed to descend into the water at the autumn equinoxes; at the vernal equinoxes, it leaves the water and ascends into the sky. It rises on the wind and the clouds, and its very breath condenses to form the rain—not only the gentle rains of the spring and autumn, but the fierce storms that make rivers overflow their banks. The dragon's spiral path to the highest heavens forms tornadoes, whirlwinds, and waterspouts. Here, dragons are the symbol of water, the symbol of life. In contrast, the Western dragon is the dragon of fire. The one ability all Western dragons have in common is their ability to breathe out smoke and fire. Their eyes, too, are usually red and furious. Because of its union with fire, the Western dragon is associated with death and the subterranean world.

Just like the free and elegant flow of water, the Chinese dragon has the Taoist freedom to do nothing gracefully and do everything elegantly. Confucius once compared Lao Tzu with the dragon, a symbol of mystery and sagacity, of aspiring deep thought and high nobility, the combination of water's flexibility and the sage's ability.

> Nothing under heaven
> Is softer and weaker than water,
> Yet nothing can compare with it
> In attacking the hard and strong.
> Nothing can change place with it.
> That the weak overcomes the strong,
> And the soft overcomes the hard,
> No one under heaven does not know,
> Though none can put it into practice.
> Therefore a sage said:
> "One who receives the filth of a state

Is called the Master of the Altar of the Soil and Grain;
One who shoulders the evils of a state
Becomes the king under heaven."
Straightforward words appear to be their reverse.
(Chen, *The Tao Te Ching,* Chapter 78)

The Qing Dynasty Cloud Dragon playing with a pearl.

We have only one moon, and no rings, but we have water.

No celestial bodies that we know of have liquid water. Intelligent beings from other planets that have no water must think we are mad with happiness to be surrounded by blue oceans and rushing rivers.

Very few people realize how fortunate we are and enjoy this beautiful world full of water. Even though Lao Tzu didn't have the knowledge of the earth's uniqueness as a ball covered with water, he finds that water represents all aspects of goodness and happiness. He believes that "the highest good is like water. Water gives life to the ten thousand things and does not strive." If we behave like water, we will be happy.

The great ocean sends us drifting like a raft, the running river sweeps us along like a reed. We do not tell the ocean to stop its tides, and we do not tell the river to flow slower. We just join them to celebrate the existence of happiness and freedom. We let water carry us to a new adventure.

12 Calm Down

How high is your blood pressure? Some people have been found to suffer from what doctors call "white coat hypertension." The doctor, believing that the hospital environment makes some people nervous enough to artificially raise their blood pressure, will help the patient to calm down, perhaps telling the patient to sit quietly and do nothing for a few minutes, or even sending the patient to rest in a darkened room. The second blood pressure reading will, of course, be lower. So which measurement represents the real blood pressure? Can patient and doctor really ignore the first, high reading? Are you usually as tense and nervous as you might be when you first enter the doctor's office? Or do you really "do nothing" all day, like the doctor had you do to calm you down? White coat hypertension notwithstanding, the first high measurement is probably closer to your true blood pressure, because most people do not allow themselves to calm down in daily life.

Unfortunately, we do not allow ourselves to do nothing during the day, even for a little while. We are constantly restless, which leads to higher blood pressure. We endlessly act and worry all our lives, except for some special moments, such as when we are checked for blood pressure. If we know that this calmness, this doing-nothing, can help us during the physical examination, why do we not perform it from time to time: not for the doctor, but for our arteries? In our daily life, we can relieve our stress-induced hypertension by creating a quiet inner corner—a self-created serene environment. We may let the day become a flowing meditation. Why do we only lie down and do nothing while sleeping during the night? We may have a short nap or powernap during the day. Why can we only calm down while listening to music? We may let the music from heaven echo through our soul. Why do we realize our humble limitations only while listening to sermons? We may give up the desire to control and let the divine universe take its course. Why do we not take time to do nothing when we have nothing to do? Rabindranath Tagore said, "Let my doing nothing when I have nothing to do become untroubled in its depth of peace like the evening on the seashore when the water is silent."[5]

You are not likely to have high blood pressure if, after a busy working day, you can see the afterglow of sunset at the margin of starry silence, if you can smell the fragrance of flowers after a bad storm, and if you can listen to honking geese head south for the winter after a busy autumn. The relaxation can be as short as ten minutes every day, or one minute every hour, or one second during a ten-minute task. The world will be diffcrent, because you are different after the relaxation.

Year in and year out, your body becomes a walking auto-biography, telling acquaintances and passersby alike of the trivial and major stresses of your life. Stress can come from many places—finances, health, job, or family issues. Salt, fat, and lack of exercise will raise your blood pressure; physical or emotional stress only add to that.

High blood pressure was the necessary response of our primitive ancestors to pump extra oxygen to their vital organs when they faced predators or cold weather. In the age of hunting and gathering, our ancestors led a quiet life. They picked berries, drank water, hunted rabbits during the day, and slept peacefully under the stars at night. However, when another tribe or a saber-toothed tiger invaded their territory, they were faced with life-or-death decisions. Primitive man had two instincts when faced with danger: to fight or to run. In either case, he didn't have the time or necessity to consider whether or not to act. There was no obstacle between stimulus and response. He belonged to nature.

We are not too different from our ancestors.

Modern man still has the same two instincts, but he is not always able to act on them. When his boss yells at him for a wrong report, he cannot kick him (although tempting) or jump out of the window (also tempting).

Modern man's response to stress is just like the caveman's. His pancreas cranks out a lot of insulin, his blood pressure rises very high, and his blood sugar shoots up to prepare for an action that he ultimately cannot take. He cannot fight or fly; he cannot kick his boss or jump out the window. Instead, he usually responds by becoming frustrated, angry, and maybe depressed.

Most of our problems do not merit the full fight-or-flight response. The high blood pressure to heighten physical alertness is not as necessary in modern life as it was in prehistoric times. If your mind continually feels stressed out, your body may maintain an abnormally high level of responsiveness, creating an artificially induced state of high blood pressure. Modern life needs a third mode, beyond the first one (fight) and the second one (flight). This third mode is nonaction. Instead of punishing ourselves for the mistakes of others, we should do nothing. That is, we should either ignore the situation, because we cannot control it, or do everything by following the course of nature.

Instead of worrying, modern man can walk out of his cramped office and watch the flowers grow, hear the birds sing, or gaze at the stars shining. He can do everything as nature does, because he is in this world for only a short visit. He does not have to solve the problems of his immediate surroundings, a limited environment that temporarily constrains him, just as he cannot solve the problems of the explosion of stars or the disappearance of a black hole. Yet he can fly with the stars, float with the clouds, and swim with the fish. If you cannot defeat the universe, you can join the universe. This is doing everything while doing nothing.

Your doctor tells you to calm down while you have your blood pressure measured. Relax, think nothing and do nothing, the doctor orders. You follow the doctor's order and can really bring your blood pressure down for the sake of the measurement. In this short period of time, you isolate yourself from the daily reality of your finances, health, job, and family. You give yourself a spiritual Shangri-la because you want to see your "real health situation." As a matter of fact, what you see is not your normal situation but your potential. Your real health situation is the first measurement, before you calmed down, when you were under the daily pressure. The measurement once you have calmed down shows your potential: you can create a Shangri-la among the daily sound and fury by taking a break or doing nothing for a moment. Unfortunately, many of us have not realized our potential to think of nothing. We think of our life as an unbroken chain: Every link in the chain is supposed to be connected to our ultimate goal in life, such as the American Dream of a house with three garages. A single error in daily life—a forgotten number, a missed appointment, an overcharged bill, a supercilious look by the boss, an awkward joke by a colleague, or a low school grade—would all supposedly impact the goal in our blueprint of life. Therefore, any event—big or small, real or imagined—causes us tension and raises our blood pressure.

One of my favorite American sayings is, "Give me a break." By saying this, we ask to be left alone from repeated pressures. "Give me a break" is an urgent plea for a pause, a rest, a cherished bit of respite. Unfortunately, while we often urge others, we do not give ourselves a break. We cannot break the self-designed chain linking everything together. We cannot pause, even for a minute, because we connect every minute with our daily bread, our life's goal, or our personal identity. We do not have the courage to take a link out of the chain. We do not have the confidence to give ourselves a hiatus in which we can stop thinking and ease our hypertension. We are not able to hold back the wheel of life to smell the fragrant flower by the road, watch the blue sky above, or talk to a passing dog, because we assume these pauses would cause us to lag behind and let our competitors pass us. We hear a cold, inimical voice reverberating: "All eyes to the front as you pass the other competitors! You do not deserve a break!"

We believe this voice. It seems we do not deserve a break as long as we have a dream. Ironically, another American dream is to retire at 50. In order to have a long break, or reside permanently in the Shangri-la of doing nothing at 50, many workers refuse to give themselves a break any time before the goal is realized. As a result, between the ages of 30 and 50, their systolic blood pressure rises 3 mmHg per year, their diastolic, 1 mmHg per year. They retire at 50, if they are lucky enough to live that long, with a blood pressure of 180 over 100.

We know how to calm down when we have our blood pressure measured. Instructed by the doctor, we can practice focusing on feeling calm. We can produce a state of relaxation that reduces heart rate, slows breathing, and lowers blood pressure. Yet we often shy away from practicing calmness because it feels artificial. We just calm down for a moment to cheat the blood pressure meter. Why do we not do ourselves a favor and have a lucid awareness of calmness a few times during the day? Why do we not pause to have a minute meditation every hour, involving deliberate breathing and sitting quietly, not for the blood pressure meter but for ourselves, not for the doctor but for our dear ones. The earth will not stop rotating if we focus on a pleasurable image, sound, or mantra, just to give ourselves a break and try to let all thoughts, feelings, sounds, and images just pass through our minds.

Many of the ways people control their stress or mask it—like eating, drinking alcohol, and smoking—contribute to the development of high blood pressure. You may wish to exercise to manage your stress. Exercise is a healing break from the chain of life. It provides your body with well-controlled physical relief. Since we usually cannot fight or fly in modern society, we use exercise as a physical substitute. However, we should also remember nonaction in this beneficial physical action. Pause and moderation are a matter of life and death for exercisers. Excessive physical stress does not benefit your circulatory system. Rather it increases your risk of illness and even death. Exercise is a marvelous antidote to pressures. However, excessive doses of an antidote can also result in injury to health. Every man is the builder of a temple: it's called a body. We should not pollute it with smoke or junk food, but neither should we overburden it and let it collapse prematurely.

In the past decade, I have been saddened by the sudden and premature deaths of my "proactive" friends. Their lives may have been entirely different. It struck me that they had one thing in common: they enjoyed strenuous or competitive exercise. Many of them were men who did sports such as marathons, lap swimming, mountain climbing, and baseball. Many of them overdid their favorite athletic activity, sometimes days or hours before their death. Many of them could have lived years longer if they had known how to exercise in moderation. It is correct to say life depends on movement. As Confucius said, "Going too far is as bad as not going far enough." Similarly, Lao Tzu said:

> Nature speaks little.
> Hence a squall lasts not a whole morning,
> A rainstorm continues not a whole day.
> What causes these?
> Heaven and earth.
> Even [the actions of] heaven and earth do not last long,
> How much less [the works] of humans?
> (Chen, *The Tao Te Ching*, Chapter 23)

Let us bellow to our middle-aged friends: Stop, pause, idle, do nothing on the edge of fatigue. Even engineers describe how metal reaches its limit and becomes stressed. You are humans of flesh and blood. Mind your "hypertension"—the word says it all.

NOTES

4.   Rabindranath Tagore, *Stray Birds*, (Old Chelsea Station, NY: Cosimo Classics, 2004) poem #208.

13 Serenity and Health

The best way to let nature follow its course is to be healthy. Every day, you replace a certain percentage of your cells. When you are optimistic, your body releases specific substances that move through your blood, telling your cells to grow and reproduce. A serene and merry mind seems to do nothing, but it sends out signals telling the cells to do everything. Exercise is like thinking with the body. Instead of receiving signals from the mind, exercises—especially noncompetitive exercises like swimming, Tai Chi, and Yoga—make your body send back healthy signals to the mind.

We are built to move, and emotion reinforces our system. Exercise triggers the signaling system that tells our mind to be calm, to stop agonizing. As a result, the mind sends "go ahead" signals to cells for the daily processes of cell replacement. Thus, the sound mind builds on a sound body, and the sound body on a sound mind. Together, they create a healthy balance of doing nothing and doing everything. So to a certain extent, your mind decides whether your cells will be healthy.

As I see it, good signals tell your cells that living is worthwhile, and healthy cells are in demand; bad signals tell your cells that reproduction is not necessary, and the existing cells can decay. Stress is the suppressed intention to act, the mentality of not allowing yourself to do nothing in the face of dangers that threatened your physical security in the past or your financial or social safety now. Long-term stress, worry, and regret produce a steady trickle of chemicals that cause your cells to neglect their long-term health to keep you wired for short-term action, in effect telling your cells to decay over time. Depression threatens your life not only through suicide but also with the cell-damaging effects of worrying. Most suicidal people do not physically commit suicide, but a suicidal mentality can terminate the body just as effectively. The mind can kill the body slowly and subconsciously. This slow dying can be reversed.

To be healthy, follow the course of nature, find a better way of living, and liberate yourself from the chains of imagined responsibility. Be generous with yourself. It is not a crime to do nothing when you do not know what to do. A typical theme in traditional Chinese painting is the fisherman returning home. His boat may be full or empty, but he is serene and healthy because he has done his day's work, and he will have nothing to do now, except let the ripple touch his boat, the breeze caress his face, and the sun set.

Nature is the great healer. Stare at it with curious eyes and know your limitations; breathe it with an empty belly, and immerse yourself in limitlessness, contemplate it with humble appreciation, and liberate yourself from unnatural bonds. Tell nature, "I trust you," and nature will not fail to give you surprises. Allow nature to embrace you, and nature will take your unhealthy mentality away and return you a calm mind and a rejuvenated body.

A day's work is done, a fisherman returns to his cottage
behind the willow trees.

14 Eating

To pursue learning, one increases daily.
To pursue Tao, one decreases daily.
To decrease and again to decrease,
Until one arrives at not doing.
Not doing and yet nothing is not done.
Always take the empire when there are no businesses.
If there are businesses,
It is not worthwhile to take the empire.
(Chen, *The Tao Te Ching*, Chapter 48)

The Taoists see food as an essential key to achieving health and longevity. They have a tendency to reduce and simplify food (Wu Wei) and another tendency to explore the world to find the healthiest food and herbs (Wu Bu Wei).

Taoists "do everything" by seeking out all kinds of natural herbs to preserve life. We can find a hermit's practice of gathering herbs in the beautiful Tang poem by Jia Dao (779–843 CE):

Seeking but Not Finding the Hermit

Under pine trees
I ask the boy;

he says: "My master's gone
to collect herbs.

I know that
he's on this mountain,

but the clouds are too deep
to know where."

Hidden deep in the cloudy and misty mountains, ginseng, ginger, and flowers join together to give us endless blessings for health and longevity. Healthy food may not always be delicious. Bitter and dry ginger may not be as tasty as a thick and juicy Big Mac. However, Mark Twain was right: "The only way to keep your health is to eat what you don't want, drink what you don't like, and do what you'd rather not." Lao Tzu tells us to "regard the great as small, the much as little" (*Tao Te Ching*, Chapter 63). The small, the few, and the tasteless can make life more healthy and tasteful.

Besides gathering herbs, the ancient Taoists created mineral medicines through alchemy, using a combination of pharmacological and spiritual techniques. Alchemy, the extreme example of doing everything, was originally an attempt at longevity in China, but it became a mysterious practice to create gold in Europe during the Middle-Ages and later transformed into chemistry during the Industrial Revolution. This practice of Wu Bu Wei is the ancestor of modern chemistry and pharmacology. The Taoists did everything imaginable to find an elixir to extend life.

Chinese emperors were notorious for having everything in life, but they had a common fear of everything that represented death. The first emperor of the Qin Dynasty defeated all his enemies in rival kingdoms and unified China in 221 BCE. After all this, he began to be haunted by his last and invincible enemy—death. When the court sorcerer, Xu Fu, persuaded him that there was elixir for life in the East, the Emperor sent him to the eastern seas twice to look for the magic drug. Xu Fu's two journeys took place between 219 BCE and 210 BCE. It was believed that his fleet included 60 ships and around 5,000 crew members, plus 3,000 virgin boys and girls. Xu Fu never returned after he embarked on a second mission in 210 BCE. Historical records suggest that he may have landed and later died in Japan. Despite his convincing argument for an elixir, Xu Fu died. The Japanese built a temple in his honor.

The first Emperor may have been too greedy and Xu Fu too cunning, but the ambition to live forever has never died in China. The Chinese Taoists are probably the people most stubborn in their belief that human beings can challenge death and disease by doing everything as well as nothing. We should adopt this spirit of persistence to achieve health and longevity. The secret was already discovered by the ancient sages: you are what you eat. You can be healthy if you consume healthy food and healthy medicine.

In Taoism, food and medicine are interchangeable. People should absorb nutritious food—such as fish, fruit and vegetables—in their bodies, supplemented by healing herbs, Tai Chi, and meditation. Traditionally, Taoist and Buddhist hermits ate very little or stopped eating at noon. Some of them ate wild berries and drank from clear springs (and fairies only sipped dew). It is a Taoist ambition to someday give up food and avoid the contamination from the "red dust" of the earth.

Zhuangzi imagined that on the mysterious mountains, there live divine immortals whose skin is white like snow, whose grace is like that of a virgin, who eat no grain and live on air and dew. They ride on clouds with flying dragons, roaming beyond the limits of the mortal realms. When time matures, the immortals can ward off corruption from all things and yield nourishing crops. We understand that people cannot live on air and dew. However, this ancient idea reveals an early awareness of the danger of overeating, even in a time when food was not as plentiful as it is today.

Lao Tzu realized the danger of luxury in eating and drinking:

> The five colors blind a person's eyes;
> the five musical notes deafen a person's ears;
> the five flavors ruin a person's taste buds.
> Horse-racing, hunting, and chasing
> drive a person's mind to madness.
> Hard-to-get goods
> hinder a person's actions.
> (Chen, *The Tao Te Ching*, Chapter 12)

Therefore, Taoism, while incorporating Wu Bu Wei to lengthen life with healthy food and medicine, also advocates constraint, or Wu Wei, in eating. Lao Tzu said, "In Tao, you should reduce something every day." Generally, modern people become obsessed with accumulating and only apply the philosophy of reducing when they want to lose weight. Modern people hate to lose anything; the only thing that they like to lose is weight. Unfortunately, the crusade to lose weight has not been successful in creating healthy eating habits.

When bored or depressed, people tend to eat too much; they do this to kill time, but in doing so, they also kill themselves. Our bodies should be sacred temples; food should be a holy sacrifice. Yet the sacred temple of the body is often offered garbage. People accumulate, and they put more and more stuff in the temple. Modern Americans have a dream: to have a house with a two- or three-car garage. However, if you walk down the street of a typical American town and peep into an open garage, you see that two thirds of that garage is filled with junk. This is like the modern person's body: commercial fullness replaces the Taoist emptiness.

As a result, two thirds of Americans are overweight or obese. I have a friend who is both nearsighted and forgetful. Every time he flies to America, he forgets his eyeglasses at home and cannot read the flight information. Luckily, he can always find the line of Americans in the airport. He just looks for the lines composed of tall, heavy ladies and gentlemen. He always identifies the correct line.

The World Health Organization (WHO) says that

Americans are the most obese people in the world. This may be because most Americans have not heard of the Taoist philosophy of constraint or Lao Tzu's saying, "In the pursuit of Tao, every day something is dropped." At the same time, many Chinese have simply forgotten their ancestors' teachings. The Chinese are catching up very quickly in their economy and, unfortunately, in their eating style as well. By 2008, more than 25 percent of the Chinese were declared overweight. It would be a nightmare if the traditional image of a slim, old Chinese sage sitting on an anchorless boat was replaced by a middle-aged, fat businessman driving a huge, Chinese-made Buick. Modern Chinese and Americans both should heed the ancient lessons, echoing from 2500 years ago, and control their desires for excessive amounts of food.

On the other hand, according to the WHO, one third of the world population is underfed and another third is starving. In such a dire and ironic situation, Lao Tzu's wisdom is like an arrow hitting the center of the target:

> The way of heaven,
> is it not like stretching a bow?
> What is high up is pressed down,
> what is low down is lifted up;
> what has surplus is reduced,
> what is deficient is supplemented.
> The way of heaven,
> it reduces those who have surpluses
> to supplement those who are deficient.
> (Chen, *The Tao Te Ching*, Chapter 77)

May the Tao of heaven conquer the way of men, and may the spirit of health and fairness permeate each corner of our unbalanced earth.

In the hunting, gathering, and farming eras of human history, people had to accumulate food, because they consumed a lot for hard labor, and they did not know when the next meal would be. This lack of food reliability is still a fact for one-third of the world's population, living in poor countries today. On the other hand, another third of modern people, who live in consumerist cultures, do not require as much food in their sedate lifestyles. Their habits lag behind their improved conditions, as they still maintain the mentality of accumulating food for hard labor and the future. For them, Lao Tzu's philosophy is again useful: "To hold and fill (a vessel) to the full, it had better not be done. To temper and sharpen a sword, its edge could not be kept long" (Chen, *The Tao Te Ching*, Chapter 9).

You will not die of thirst if you do not fill your cup to the brim. Instead, if it is too full, you may spill everything. Those who have too much must pour some of their fortune into the cups of those who have not enough to benefit the health and longevity of all. Food, the miracle cause of both life and death, should manifest itself as an equalizer between the hungry and the overfed, the meeting place for Wu Wei and Wu Bu Wei.

15 Sleeping

One thing closely related to eating is sleeping. When we sleep, our subconscious examines our daily activities, including our eating habits, because during sleep we are more alone, sensitive, and vulnerable. In my hometown there is an old folk saying: "One less bite of supper gives you a whole night of comfort." If the farmers found such a truth when food was scarce, this saying will surely be more applicable to the present world, where one third of the population overeats.

Eating both rewards and punishes sleep. The best time to know whether you are eating the right amount is usually when you half wake up at midnight or dawn. You will realize then if you have eaten too much, because this is the time of day that you are most sensitive to your previous day's behavior. Unfortunately, the feelings at this time are often depressed into the subconscious, and when the daytime comes again, we may repeat the excessive lifestyle by forgetting our body's sensitivity. Remembering the message of Wu Wei during sleep is good guidance during the daytime.

When we talk about life, we focus on our waking lives, but sleep takes up one third of our time. Shakespeare said that sleep is the chief nourisher of life's feast. In his eyes, sleep is the preparation for our waking life. As a matter of fact, sleep itself is a part of life.

In sleep, one has an endless depth of blackness to sink into. Daylight is too shallow; it will not be able to bear the heavy burden of sleep. Quality of sleep is as important as the quality of waking time, and the health of sleep is just as important as health when we are awake. People enjoy or suffer a lot during sleep, just as much as during the day, even though they do not always remember it. Sleep, doing absolutely nothing, allows the body to rejuvenate and repair itself for tomorrow's work, the work of doing everything.

It takes a lot of effort to enter the realm of doing nothing. Half of the population suffers from insomnia. In most cases, insomnia is just anxiety against doing nothing. They are worried that they are wasting time by lying awake. Most people cannot do nothing while awake and keep worrying about their daytime life. Some people feel that it is a disaster to enter the realm most close to death. They fight with the pillow and cannot kick their worries out of bed. When asked about a cure for insomnia, Mark Twain said, "Try lying on the edge of the bed, then you might drop off." There is wisdom in this pun: when we go to sleep, we need the courage to let go, even with the risk of falling off the edge. We should be like Huck Finn drifting down the Mississippi River, and say firmly to life, "I believe in you. Just give us what you have."

In most languages, sleeping like a baby is the best kind of sleep. At the same time, when we sleep, we allow ourselves to do everything—such as flying, chasing or being chased by a monster, saying what we would not dare to say, and experiencing what we would not dare to experience. That is dreaming. Deep sleep, deep nonaction, lets us dream and allows us to cleanse our nervous system of toxic stress and anxiety. Sleep is the best expression of doing nothing. An unknown author called consciousness "that annoying time between naps."

We do not understand our existence, but we can acknowledge the limits of our understanding. As long as you understand your limitations, you are able to surpass them. Zhuangzi often writes about withdrawal from the numerous into the one as a detachment from the whole world of multiplicity. One's mind ventures into a lonely place beyond the reach of life and death. It is the Taoist dream to find a kingdom between life and death. An active sleep, a positive meditation, is closest to this realm, a land where one can move freely between doing nothing and doing everything and reach a kind of liberation from selfhood that triumphs over death. Joy and sorrow are alternatives, like day and night, like birth and death. There is an ecstasy between life and death that can be experienced as we fall asleep every night. When we go rambling without a destination, enjoying the joy of soaring above the realm of conventional concerns and practical judgments, the universe expands, the world goes on; somebody creates goodness somewhere, and someone commits an evil somewhere, but we have found the courage to sleep and solve our problems later.

Zhuangzi once dreamed he was a butterfly. In shape and in mood, he really felt like a butterfly. He did not know Zhuangzi at all. Suddenly he woke up, and really felt he was Zhuangzi. He did not know whether he was Zhuangzi dreaming that he was a butterfly or a butterfly dreaming that he was Zhuangzi.

Nevertheless, sleep is not that easy for everybody. Every night, a billion people in the world will stop breathing during sleep, some for a few seconds, some for a few minutes. Snoring results from the repetitive closure of the airway. These people suffer from a sleep disorder called sleep apnea, but unfortunately, 90 percent of those who have it do not know that they suffer from it, and even fewer seek treatment. There are many treatments for this disease, from air-pumping machines (CPAPs) to dental devices to surgery. People should do everything to find a treatment in order to be able to do nothing—and sleep.

Sleep apnea causes fatigue, damages the cardiovascular system, and disrupts family harmony. Sleep, for those who suffer from sleep apnea, is a nightmare. The victims forget it the next day, but their fatigue, irritation, and clumsiness during waking hours tell the world how they have suffered. When Edgar Allen Poe said, "Sleep: those little slices of death! How I loathe them!" he revealed that he might have suffered from sleep apnea. For sleep apnea patients, falling asleep is like falling dead with suffocation every night, but fortunately, most of them do not remember the experience the next morning.

Since the transition between sleep and waking is like that between life and death, we often feel very lonely when we fall asleep. In most languages, sleeping with someone means having sexual relations with them. However, to sleep with somebody requires more love than sexual relations, because in falling asleep, you enter an unknown world. This voyage requires the best company you can find. In the Peking opera "Legend of White Snake," a boatman sings to a couple who are falling in love. He sings, "You have to have ten lives of good behavior for you to take the same boat together once. You have to have 100 lives of good behavior to share the same pillow."

The moon's beams dance, the stream's ripples sing a lullaby, and the time to sleep has come.

16

Do Nothing, Only Breathe

In bringing your spiritual and bodily souls to embrace the One,
Can you never depart from it?
In concentrating your breath to attain softness,
Can you be like an infant?
(Chen, *The Tao Te Ching*, Chapter 10)

The first thing you did in life was what? Breathe. The last thing you will do before you leave this world is what? Breathe. Lao Tzu often says to forget everything, so we must relearn how to breathe.

The best things in life are free. Air, so far, is free. Breathwork is not only the least expensive activity, it is also the most effective healing exercise. Breath represents the movement of energy in the body. Life begins with breathing and ends with breathing. Unfortunately, most people perform this birthright in the wrong way: too shallowly, too passively, too irregularly, and too unconsciously.

Proper breathing is the key to self-healing and anxiety control, providing astonishing cures by our mind for our body. There is not much you can do to control your heart or stomach or bowels, but you can use your lungs either consciously or unconsciously, deliberately or automatically.

Lungs are double-directed; they're the link between the conscious and the unconscious. The most beautiful places in the world are the places where two phenomena meet: the seashore, where the ocean splashes the sand, the riverbanks, where water splashes the earth. Breathing can be the most beautiful function of our body, because in breathing, the conscious touches the unconscious. You can establish ways of breathing that make your voluntary nervous system affect your involuntary nervous system. In breathing, the two worlds of doing everything and doing nothing touch each other and produce transparent sparks, shining over our often dark and anxious minds. You can do everything to change the rhythm and depth of your breath; you can do nothing and let the universe breathe through you.

In Chinese, breath or qi (chi) represents energy, spirit, and life. The Confucian philosopher Mencius declared, "I am prone to nurture my broad breath." Taoist philosopher Zhuangzi, advocating the deepest breath possible, imagined immortals who could breathe from their heels. They all believed that breathwork can lift your spirit.

Your breath is the most important tool you have to control your mind. Emotional stress can constrict muscles all over your body, including your neck, shoulders, and chest. The constriction can limit your lungs' capability to expand when you inhale, so you take quick and shallow breaths that fill only the upper part of your lungs. This leads to a shortage of oxygen, as if you were at the top of a high mountain. Lack of oxygen causes stress, irritation, and anxiety. The converse is also true: when you are stressed, irritated, or anxious, you breathe fast and shallowly. The faster you breathe, the more upset you are; the slower you breathe, the more tranquil you are; the deeper you breathe, the calmer you are. Shallow and quick breath is the invisible assassin of your mind and body.

Many people know how to relax at any given moment: take a few long, deep breaths in and out. However, few know a more effective remedy: breathe abdominally when you breathe in. In belly breathing, when you breathe in, you still lower the diaphragm, but the ribs stay still, instead of going up. When you inhale, expand your belly rather than your chest. You still expand your lungs, but your focus is lower.

When we were more like other animals, we used four limbs to move around. Four million years ago, we stood up and walked on two legs: we became different from every other animal. Everything human is vertical and tall. We must look very funny to other animals! Now, when we belly-breathe, we reverse; everything is lower. We are returning to our origins, to a lower space that is closer to the earth, as when we walked (crawled) on our four limbs. The lower focus of belly breathing will reverse the human tendency to grow higher all the time. The more advanced, higher, and straighter position has

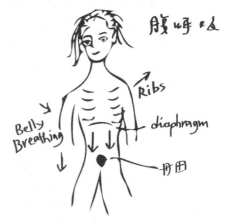

some side effects, such as high blood pressure, and back and neck pain.

To learn belly breathing, place a hand on your abdomen and take a slow and deep breath, imagining that your belly is an empty lake that you are filling with clear water through the river that flows through your respiratory tract. Your hand should rise when you inhale and fall when you exhale.

Belly breathing is how people normally breathe when they are relaxed; when people are stressed, they resort to laborious chest-breathing. For too many people, relaxation is not the normal state of mind; for them, chest breathing has become the "normal" way to breathe. Through practice, you can train yourself to breathe from the belly, even when you do not pay attention to it. You can return to natural and healthy breathing. Breathing this way will massage your spine from the inside; no massage from the outside will be able to do that. If you can breathe like this even when you are stressed, you reach the goal of doing nothing while doing everything. You beat the stress.

Prolonged stress contributes to many different illnesses. Stress depresses your immune system, raises your blood pressure, and strains your sanity. By learning to center the mind and make our breathing work more effectively, we can neutralize stress so that it will not damage our bodies. To relieve stress, some people indulge in smoking, gambling, and illegal drugs. By doing these things, people wish to center the mind and do nothing. Actually, they are doing something—something that is damaging to health and economically unrewarding, something that they will regret later. Proper breathing, on the other hand, is healthy, free, and impossible to regret.

In breathing, emptiness is more important than fullness. People seem to think and behave otherwise. They fill and overfill everything, including a practice as simple as a breath. Watch how people breathe. You will find most of them make efforts to inhale but none to exhale. Common sense seems to support that exhalation is passive and inhalation is active. When you breathe with this "common sense," you do not move enough air in and out of your lungs. Remedy: put emptiness above fullness. Squeeze out more air and empty your lungs. You take care of the exhale part; let inhale take care of itself. Most swimming coaches tell their swimmers to exhale thoroughly before they inhale. Try to make your exhalation as long and smooth as possible. Combine this exhaling with belly breathing. Your hand on the belly should feel the belly fall deeply while you exhale and rise high while you inhale, just as tides rise and fall. "What are you doing?" people may ask you. "Nothing," you answer. People still breathe while doing nothing, do they not? You really do nothing between exhale and inhale.

A yawn extends the transition between inhale and exhale: it's a deep breath with the mouth open, a stretch of the body, a contraction of the tongue, a pause against the process of life, a break against daily boredom. It's a demonstration of our body's wish for Wu Wei. Belly breathing, like yawning, is nonaction, giving your body a break; but this time, it is nonaction of the chest.

During the transition, you take a brief pause between breathing in and breathing out. You may extend the transition to give your respiratory system a break. As a matter of fact, you are also doing everything: you find the breath of the universe, you resume the cycle of life, and you wander in the world of infinity.

Changing from chest breathing to belly breathing is a reversal. Everything reversed is a new opportunity. Your ribs have been moving the wrong way all your life, but now they can rest.

17 Learning

In the present world, we drown in information and starve for knowledge. We drown in expertise and starve for wisdom. Information includes facts and data; knowledge makes facts and data relevant. Expertise seeks answers to every question; wisdom rests at the juncture between us and our question. Rainer Maria Rilke warns us, "Do not seek answers, which cannot be given to you. The most important thing is to experience everything. Live the questions now." We should be patient towards all that is unanswered in our heart, and to try to love the questions themselves.

An ancient wise man's knowledgeable
discovery on an innocent stone.

From knowing to not knowing,
This is superior.
From not knowing to knowing,
This is sickness.
It is by being sick of sickness
That one is not sick.
The sage is not sick.
Because he is sick of sickness,
Therefore he is not sick.
(Chen, *The Tao Te Ching*, Chapter 71)

Confucius said something similar: "To know something is to know it; not to know something is not to know it. That is knowledge." Socrates also said: "I'm more intelligent than others simply because I know that I am ignorant."

Assuming to know what you do not leads to evil. Recognize your ignorance and know your limits. When a common person thinks he is knowledgeable when he is ignorant, he is funny or even adventurous. When a person with power thinks he is knowledgeable when he is ignorant, he can cause terrible destruction. Evil is ignorance plus power.

It would seem, then, that the best way to avoid evil is to learn. Confucius believed this, and traditional Chinese culture seems to be built on the idea that the only people qualified to lead are the scholars. Lao Tzu dared to challenge this tradition:

Eliminate learning so as to have no worries.
Yes and no, how far apart are they?
Good and evil, how far apart are they?

Learning

> What the sages fear,
> I must not not fear.
> I am the wilderness before the dawn.
> The multitude are busy and active,
> Like partaking of the sacrificial feast,
> Like ascending the platform in spring;
> I alone am bland,
> As if I have not yet emerged into form.
> Like an infant who has not yet smiled,
> Lost, like one who has nowhere to return.
> (Chen, *The Tao Te Ching*, Chapter 20)

Lao Tzu promotes contradiction and reversal, but is he really against knowledge?

We can understand him on three levels:

First, some scholars say that "give up" is the wrong translation from the Chinese. They prefer: *With extreme studies, you will have no worries.*

Second, some see studies as referring to established, Confucian forms of learning: *Give up scrupulous studies, and you will have no worries.*

The third is a more literal understanding: *Give up all learning, and you will have no worries.*

The second translation, the compromise, is easier for us to understand, but Lao Tzu is clearly saying that we should give up knowledge completely. Our troubles start from knowledge: when we analyze things, when we try to control our fate, when we play the ruler of the universe, we get into trouble. Can we really give up all study? Not really. Lao Tzu is overcorrecting.

These graduates follow *Tao Te Ching* literally
and have abandoned learning.

In the following picture, a little girl is running towards the
target. Every direction she takes is wrong. First, she aims too
far to the left—that is wrong. She runs too far to the right—
wrong again. In the end, she reaches the target because she
keeps correcting herself: left to right, right to left. Each correction helps her to approach the target. We do this kind of
thing every day of our lives. To drive straight, we must turn
the wheel a few degrees to the left, a few degrees to the right,
and back again every moment.

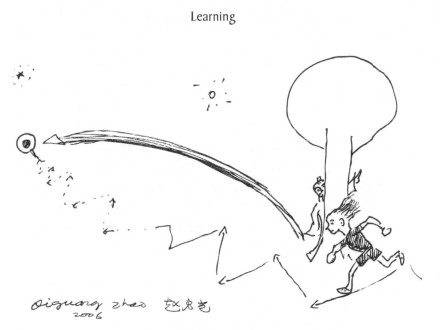

Qiguang zhao 赵启光
2006

Every direction is wrong,
but every correction brings you closer to the goal.

When our car slips on ice and swerves to the left, we turn
the steering wheel hard to the right, even though we only want
to keep going straight. If we refused to do this, we would drive
into a ditch. We cannot help it if we do the wrong things, say
the wrong words, and get the wrong ideas. Yet we keep correcting our deeds, words, and ideas to reach our goals. To "stay the
course" and refuse to correct ourselves would be disastrous!
We move in numerous sub-directions that keep going to their
opposites. Every direction is wrong, but we correct ourselves
by reversing, self-denying, or self-correcting. When we are facing in the right direction, we must turn the wheel back to the
left again and straighten out. We reach our goals by a series of
mistakes, a series of continuous, self-reversing mistakes.

When a bike rider turns left at the edge of a gulf, we shout "Right!" although the correct direction is front. When Lao Tzu tells us to abandon learning, he's pointing us in the wrong direction. He is still right—just make sure that you do not take his advice too far and fall off the other edge. Like the girl's zigzag path toward her target, or the back-and-forth motion of steering a car, the "correct direction" is really a series of wrong directions that cancel each other out. Lao Tzu tells us to give up all knowledge so that when we turn away from our rigid studies, we will be pointed in the right direction.

Be aware of the master's wise overcorrection
and do not fall over the other edge.

Learning

Knowledge can help us, but it can also allow us to be manipulated. When we only follow what we know, and forget to follow what we feel, we can easily be led down the wrong path. Let go of the arguments and counterarguments that confuse the matter, and make your own path.

> The five colors blind a person's eyes;
> The five musical notes deafen a person's ears;
> The five flavors ruin a person's taste buds.
> Horseracing, hunting, and chasing
> Drive a person's mind to madness.
> Hard-to-get goods
> Hinder a person's actions.
> Therefore the sage is for the belly, not for the eyes.
> Therefore he leaves this and chooses that.
> (Chen, *The Tao Te Ching*, Chapter 12)

There are too many colors in the world that distract us. Trust your mind and instincts, not superficial first impressions or artificial knowledge.

Zhuangzi told the story of a cook famous for his skill at carving oxen. He was so skilled that his movements were like a dance and the sound of his knife was like music. Prince Wenhui asked him how he could perform this task so beautifully. The cook put down his knife and answered:

> I follow the Tao, and the skill follows me. When I first began carving oxen, all I saw was the whole ox. Now, three years later, I do not see the whole ox at all. I use my spirit to see instead of my eyes. My senses may wish to stop, but the spirit

will keep going. I just follow Heaven's law.... A good cook changes his knife once a year because he cuts; a common cook changes his knife every month because he hacks. I have used my knife for nineteen years, having cut thousands of oxen, and my knife is as sharp as it was when it was new.... My knife is thin; the oxen's joints are wide. The thinness enters the wideness, and my job becomes effortless.

The cook cuts the ox so effortlessly because he understands it in pieces, and not as a whole ox. He lets his knife follow a natural course and does not care for "skill." Skill can be taught; the spiritual, the instinctive, cannot. This is also nondoing or nonlearning, because the cook does not use the knife to carve the ox; he uses nature to carve the ox. What Lao Tzu wants is to abandon the common cook's carving by fixed skills and learn the effortless talent demonstrated by the super cook. This is the true learning.

We have tons of how-to books, but we should not let them smother us. You cannot learn how to lead your life; let nature guide you, and your knife will always stay sharp.

Zhuangzi echoes Lao Tzu:

> The skillful toil, the clever worry,
> Have no abilities and you'll have no ambitions.
> Eat your fill and stroll as you please,
> Adrift like a boat loose from its moorings.[6]

Oiguay Zhou 4/2/2006

Drift like a boat loose from its moorings.

This is not to say that all skills are bad, but we should allow ourselves to wander from the fixed path. We should allow ourselves to gaze at the sky and accept that the current will shift, and our boat may not travel in the direction we first expected. When we cut ourselves loose, we are free to see the beauty around us without worrying about which harbor our boat will eventually come to rest in. When we have created a peaceful mind, it will lighten our hearts and open the door to knowledge; the light of wisdom will shine around us. If you want the world to be happy, start with being happy yourself. This is the hardest thing to learn.

When a superior person hears Tao,
He diligently practices it.
When a middling person hears Tao,
He hears it, he doesn't hear it.
When the inferior person hears Tao, he roars.
If Tao were not laughed at,
It would not be Tao.
(Chen, *The Tao Te Ching*, Chapter 41)

Taoism is for everyone, not only for us; but we are the ones who chose to grab it and make it ours. Does that make us wise students? Perhaps.

If Lao Tzu's teachings were nothing more than "common sense," nobody would laugh. However, Lao Tzu's thoughts were provocative and original; they made people uncomfortable. Conventional minds laughed Taoism off as ridiculous, but their laughter shows that Lao Tzu hit a sensitive spot. Lao Tzu called them foolish, but he knew that we need "foolish" people. His Tao would not exist without them.

Understanding is elusive. Life is short, the universe goes on, and there is a lot you will not understand. If you play the game of life well, you can make it a comedy, even if the whole thing is tragic.

NOTES

5. Zhuangzi, *The Inner Chapters*, trans. A.C. Graham (Indianapolis: Hackett Publishing Company, Inc., 2001), 142.

18 Justice

Govern a state by the normal;
Conduct warfare as the abnormal;
Take the empire when there is no business.
(Chen, *The Tao Te Ching*, Chapter 57)

According to Lao Tzu, the concept of justice incorporates elements of surprise. When you play chess, you attack by surprise. This is Wu Bu Wei, or doing everything. In your daily life, if you work under justice and fairness, you can still make surprise moves. At the same time, your soul should abide by nonaction. You understand that whatever happens may not be what you initially expect. You understand that you should not be confined by worry about the past, the present, and the future. They are beyond your control. Keep a just strategy, surprise moves, and a calm mind.

What is at equilibrium is easy to maintain;
What has not emerged is easy to plan;
What is fragile is easy to dissolve;
What is minute is easy to disperse.
Act when there is yet nothing to do.

Govern when there is yet no disorder.
A tree whose trunk is of a man's embrace,
Begins from something extremely tiny.
A tower of nine stories high
Is built from a heap of earth.
A trip of a thousand miles
Begins right at one's feet.
(Chen, *The Tao Te Ching*, Chapter 64)

I once said in class, "Do not interfere too much with the world." A student asked me, "But what do we do with evil? Do we sit around and let it happen?"

Of course, we cannot always avert disaster. When we see evils in the world, our first response is to do something. We want to take an eye for an eye and a tooth for a tooth. We consider this just and fair. We think that through action, we will quickly solve our problems. Instead, our first response should be to strengthen our sense of goodness and to ask ourselves whether violently eliminating the "evildoer" really solves the problem. We do not know that the "evildoer" is the real source of the problem, and the chain reactions to our first "Empire Strikes Back"–style response may cause chaos or retaliation. If we act without thinking, we will have to remedy all the problems we created by our action. Ideally, we should keep evil from happening at the very beginning; trouble is easily overcome before it starts.

It is often unclear whether we should meet injustice with action or with nonaction. Action is commonly considered the strong, moral option, while nonaction is thought to be weak or immoral. As a matter of fact, nonaction can be equally moral and may demand more strength and respect for justice.

After 9/11, most Americans came to see Saddam Hussein as an evil person, but the link between Saddam Hussein and 9/11 was unclear and the Iraq invasion put Iraq in turmoil. Political analysts argue about whether the United States should or should not have removed him from power, but in the future, we should consider that nonaction can be just as ideologically and morally fair as action. If we do not take action, it does not mean that we are sympathetic with evil. We should not be considered weak if we do not take immediate action. Nonaction means not to take action against nature. Human rights are one aspect of nature, so when we act for justice, we follow the course of nature. We must be sure that if we act for justice, we are not creating more problems through our actions than we would create through inaction.

19 Work and Leisure

"Never be afraid of the moments," announces the voice of the eternal. "Never be afraid of doing nothing," announces the voice of doing everything.

Let me do nothing when I have nothing to do. Let me be when I do not do. Let leisure and guilt never stroll hand in hand. Let work and pain never stride shoulder to shoulder.

Take the leisurely route and follow the course of nature.

Zhuangzi said, "To regard accumulation as deficiency, and to dwell quietly alone with the spiritual and the intelligent—herein lie the techniques of the Tao of the ancients." To earn bread is important; to taste its sweetness is more important. Richard Layard, an economist at the London School of Economics, provides one important example of work and happiness. He argues that unemployment is no longer Britain's biggest social problem. While there are many Britons unemployed, there are as many receiving disability benefits because depression and stress have left them unfit to work. Policy-minded economists such as Lord Layard are no longer satisfied with raising the rate of employment. They want to lift the rate of enjoyment too.

We like to fantasize that hard work will lead to leisure. John Keynes, the supporter of capitalism, anticipated that wealthier societies would become more leisured ones, liberated from toil to find pleasure in the finer things in life. Karl Marx, the adversary of capitalism, also predicted that the owners of productive property would enjoy leisure in culture and education. If our lives together prove half as rosy as they predict, we will be well content. Today, people work harder and more willingly to afford possessions they hope will make them happy. Ironically, people seem to overwork, especially in the United States, where Keynes is popular, and in China, where Marx is respected. People work by all the means they can, in all the ways they can, in all the places they can, at all the times they can, and as long as they can, only to discover that the fruits of their labor sour quickly. Everybody wishes for a higher place in society's pecking order, and they force others in the rat race to climb faster to keep up. As a result, everyone loses. Americans are still much like Alexis de Tocqueville discovered them in 1835: "So many lucky men, restless in the midst of abundance." The reason? They have more, but so do their neighbors. The Chinese in the twenty-first century have much more material wealth than they had decades ago, but more people become victims of "red-eye disease" (in Chinese) or "the green-eyed monster" (in English), because they see that their neighbors have more than they do.

Many of us cannot simply mind our own business; we cannot help minding other people's business either. Doing well is not sufficient. We want to beat our peers. This status anxiety runs deep in our nature. Monkeys at the top of the tree enjoy more mates and more bananas. The monkeys in the lower branches have mates and bananas, too, but they are restless, because the top monkeys have more. To occupy a higher position in the tree, many people are willing to work overtime every day. They gain in rank at the expense of their own and their colleagues' leisure time. In making that sacrifice, they also hurt anyone else who shares the status anxiety. Their coworkers must give up their free time to keep up. Many people wish to work less, if only others would do so. Yet a bargain cannot be reached unilaterally. On the contrary, the little guys are afraid of falling behind in the race, knowing that if they do not work harder, they will lose their rank to somebody who does.

Rabindranath Tagore believes that, "Leisure, in its activity, is work" (see his poem, *Stray Birds*).

Even Alan Lakein, after speaking of "mastering your time and mastering your life," suggests that we find time to relax and do nothing; we will have more fun and get more done doing it.

People could work shorter hours and commute shorter distances, even if that means living in smaller houses with cheaper gadgets. Modern people have become like Kua Fu in the ancient Chinese story. It is said that in antiquity a giant named Kua Fu was determined to have a race with the Sun. So he ran like an arrow in the direction of the Sun. Finally, he was too thirsty and hot to continue. The Yellow River came into sight, roaring on in front of him. He swooped upon it earnestly and drank up the whole river. Then he drank all the water of the Wei River. He still felt thirsty and hot, so he marched northward for the lakes. Unfortunately, when he was halfway there, he fell down and died of thirst and heat. This is the origin of the Chinese idiom, "Kua Fu chasing the Sun." It applies to someone who does something courageous but impossible to accomplish, just like Icarus, the Greek mythological figure, who flew too close to the sun with his wings of wax.

Unfortunately, there are numerous Kua Fus in the modern world. They chase the suns named Prosperity and Success without stopping. These modern sun-chasers are even more miserable than Kua Fu. While Kua Fu chased the sun alone, pausing and drinking deliberately, modern sun chasers are pressured by their fellow runners. While Kua Fu could only aim at the target in the sky, his modern followers have to aim at the same target, while also looking backward over their shoulders. Even though they are thirsty, hot, and exhausted, they cannot stop, because they see the sun moving above and

Kua Fu, the sun chaser.

the competitors catching up. In addition, many people say, "I will retire when I have worked this many years and saved this much money." Some fortunate people really reach their goal, ready to enjoy the years of leisure they have worked for all their life. Unfortunately, many die or lose their health before they can fully enjoy the fruits of their labor. Some people even die before they can retire, and some people never save that much money when they have worked that many years. The sun is still moving, but the chasers are not anymore.

Not that we should love ease and detest work. On the contrary, work is a lasting joy. Insight, ingenuity, and vigor lie in our work. The most happiness a man ever feels is the happiness of finishing his work. People are happy while reading, listening to music, and wandering around the garden, but lucky people also get satisfaction from losing themselves in their work, "forgetting themselves in a function," as W.H. Auden put it. In Auden's poem, surgeons manage this by "making a primary incision," and clerks do it when "completing a bill of lading." This state of losing oneself is just doing nothing while doing everything.

While losing ourselves in work, we take work seriously but we do not take ourselves seriously. This kind of work saves us from depression. We are invigorated by the work itself,

Mr. Lee finally moves from a cubicle to an office with a view. Unfortunately, the beauty of mountaintops reminds him of the NASDAQ charts.

instead of feeling wasted by worries about personal gains and losses. Work should provide a process instead of a goal, a sense of control instead of submission, and harmony instead of confrontation. Therefore, jogging under the rising sun gives us carefree and joyous invigoration, while chasing the sun can cause untold suffering.

Fame and Fortune

Your name and your body, which is dearer?
Your body and material goods, which is more abundant?
Gain and loss, which is illness?
Therefore in excessive love, one necessarily goes to great expenses,
In hoarding much, one necessarily loses heavily.
Knowing contentment, one does not suffer disgrace,
Knowing when to stop, one does not become exhausted.
This way one may last long.
(Chen, *The Tao Te Ching*, Chapter 44)

Liu Zongyuan, a great Chinese writer of the Tang Dynasty, was once the governor of Liuzhou. He recorded this anecdote:

The people of Liuzhou were good swimmers. One day, there was a flood, and five or six people tried to cross the river. When they were in the middle of the river, their boat began to leak. Everybody jumped into the river and started to swim. One man swam very hard, but not as well as usual. His companions yelled, "You're the best swimmer, why are you lagging behind?" He said, "I have a thousand coins wrapped around my waist. They're very heavy." His companions said, "Why do not you let them go?" He would not answer, but only shook his head. A little later, he was exhausted. Some of his companions had already reached the shore. They jumped up and down, yelling, "You idiot! You're drowning! If you die, what will you need money for?" He shook his head again and drowned.

The fish: "I hope there are more idiots like him."

Liu Zongyuan commented, "I was very sad to hear this story. He was drowned by a small fortune, but many important people are killed by bigger fortunes."

Shakespeare said in *Timon of Athens:* "Gold? Yellow, glittering, precious gold? …Thus much of this will make black white, foul fair, wrong right, base noble, old young, coward valiant." I would like to add that it can also make alive dead.

Robbers all over the world, without having to be taught, know how to use this line: "Your money or your life?" Most people would choose their life in this critical moment, but when there is no robber holding a gun to their head, they do not realize that they are facing the same life-or-death question. Like the drowning swimmer, they cannot answer Lao Tzu's question: "Self or wealth: Which is more precious?" In daily life, money lovers may not drown immediately, but the heavy load, little by little, drags them under.

If we think that the man in Liu Zongyuan's story was foolish because he would not throw away the heavy copper coins around his waist, think again: many great men in history have made exactly the same mistake. They were dragged under the water by the heavy burden of wealth and something similar: fame. As a matter of fact, there is a Chinese word that combines the concepts of fame and wealth: *mingli*. Lao Tzu severely criticized those people who sacrificed their life for *mingli*. In one breath, he asked, "Fame or self: Which matters more? Self or wealth: Which is more precious? Gain or loss: Which is more painful?"

Xiang Yu was a well-known tragic hero who lived during the end of the Qin dynasty (221 BCE–207 BCE). He was from the kingdom of Chu, which was conquered by the Qin. Taking advantage of the turmoil against the cruel Qin emperor, Xiang Yu rose to be the mightiest of the rebels who overthrew the Qin Dynasty. Among the rebel leaders was another well-known general, Liu Bang. Xiang Yu was from an aristocratic family that loved fame and ritual. Liu Bang was from a common family and was crafty and shameless. Their competition for the crown of China became a favorite topic of Chinese literature and theater.

Xiang Yu had many opportunities to capture or eliminate Liu Bang because, in the beginning, Liu Bang was much weaker. Again and again, Xiang Yu let Liu Bang go, because he did not want to look like a bully. During the most famous of these missed opportunities, Hongmen Feast, Xiang Yu forced Liu Bang to visit his camp to have a banquet with him. When Xiang Yu's mentor and chief advisor raised a jade decoration to signal Xiang Yu to arrest Liu Bang, Xiang Yu looked away. Finally, he let Liu Bang leave safe and sound, and Liu Bang grew stronger and stronger, until he drove Xiang Yu into a corner.

Ultimately, Xiang Yu was surrounded at Gaixia. His soldiers were few and his supplies were exhausted. From the top of a hill, Xiang Yu saw only lines and lines of enemy camps. At night, he heard the enemy soldiers sing the folk songs of the kingdom of Chu, his native land. He exclaimed, "Has the enemy conquered my kingdom and enlisted my young men?" Then he began to drink his last cup of wine with his concubine, Lady Yu. She was a brave woman, who had followed him from battlefield to battlefield up until that moment. He untied his favorite steed and tried to get it to leave, but it would not go away. Lady Yu said, "You often ask me to dance, and I've always refused. Now I'll do my first and last dance for you." Xiang Yu said, "I'll accompany you with my song." This song became one of the most famous Chinese poems. Its heroic and tragic tone has touched millions of people through the years:

I am strong enough to uproot the hills,
I am mighty enough to shadow the world.
But the times are against me,
And my horse will not leave.
When my horse will not leave,
What then can I do?
Oh Lady Yu, my Yu,
What will become of you?

Xiang Yu was defeated by his love of fame.

At the end of the dance, the concubine killed herself with his sword. Xiang Yu escaped to the shore of the River Wu, chased by the army of Liu Bang. A village head, who was waiting with a boat on the riverbank, said, "I beg you to make haste and cross the river, and you can raise an army to counterattack from your original base."

Xiang Yu laughed bitterly and replied, "It is Heaven that is destroying me. What good would it do me to cross the river? Once, with eight thousand sons from the land east of the river, I crossed over and marched west, but today not a single man of them returns. Although their fathers and brothers east of the river should take pity on me and make me their king, how could I bear to face them again? Though they said nothing of it, could I help but feel shame in my heart?"[7]

Raising his head, he saw the enemy marching close to him. He dismounted and drew his sword for his last fight; he killed hundreds of soldiers. Exhausted, he found an old acquaintance among the marching enemy. "I heard that Liu Bang will pay a thousand ounces of gold for my head," he said to his former friend. "I will give the honor to you." And with that, Xiang Yu cut his own throat.

Xiang Yu blamed heaven and the times for his failures, but he forgot to blame himself. He was so attached to his fame that he let his archenemy go, so attached to his fame was he that he would not return to his home town lest his countrymen should laugh at him. His attachment to fame was as solid and heavy as that of the sinking swimmer to the money around his waist.

In our daily life, we also have attachments; we take them as part of our identity and forget that we can free ourselves from the burden. We are so afraid of peer pressure and gossip that we sink and kill ourselves without knowing it. We are afraid of being criticized, and we worry about our images. Am I too fat? Am I too inefficient? Is my car fancy enough? Do people like me?

Fame and Fortune

Outside material things have become an inseparable part of our ego. Faced with the alternatives Lao Tzu offers us—wealth or self, fame or self—we often make the wrong choice unknowingly. Let Lao Tzu's prescription cure our attachment:

Therefore in excessive love, one necessarily goes to great expenses,
In hoarding much, one necessarily loses heavily.
Knowing contentment, one does not suffer disgrace,
Knowing when to stop, one does not become exhausted.
This way, one may last long.
(Chen, *The Tao Te Ching*, Chapter 44)

Modern people have more attachments than ever, such as cars, houses, and cell phones. They do not know these attachments rob them of a meaningful life. I had a friend in business who lost his cell phone containing thousands of numbers. This was a disastrous thing, because people in modern China all depend on their *guangxi*, their business and social network. If you want to get anything done, you have to know someone in your guangxi either directly or indirectly. Without guangxi, you are nobody, so naturally he was panicked, pacing up and down "like an ant on a hot wok." He did nothing the whole day. When he returned home, he walked toward his apartment building and a miracle happened: Something caught his attention that he had totally ignored before. There was a tree in front of the building that had grown tall from a sapling. He had never noticed it, because he was always calling someone on the cell phone. He entered his apartment, sat with his family for dinner, and for the first time, he was not calling someone. He looked around—who was this lady with fair gray hair around her temples? Who was this lanky teenager who used to be a toddler? They were his wife and his daughter; he had not looked at them carefully for the past 10 years. Now he stared tenderly at his family, and they looked back with smiles. A harmonious chi rose among them, like an auspicious cloud bringing back 10 years lost among thousands of telephone conversations.

For the first time he "did nothing" at home. No socializing with his friends, no negotiating with his partners, and no conspiring against his opponents. As a matter of fact, in doing nothing, he had done everything that was necessary to reconnect with his family and redefine himself. Here, gain and loss occur simultaneously. As Lao Tzu said, "Thus things are either decreased so as to be increased, or increased so as to be decreased" (*Tao Tê Ching*, Chapter 42). He lost his cell phone, but he regained something he did not realize he had lost: his family, his happiness, and his life. The whole family also regained what was lost before. Doing nothing is returning to the present, liberating oneself from the fantasy of potential gains and losses.

You do not have to throw your cell phone away to do nothing. You can do something very simple that is unconventional, something you have never done before: leave your cell phone at home, read a book in the forest, write a note to leave at the tree, stand with your arms upward for a few minutes, and look at the shining stars. There is courage in not caring what others think about your uncommon action, when you find that the greatest show in the universe is the universe. Today, you are not going to miss this show. This time, you are going to watch the stars—the great doing nothing and doing everything.

In doing nothing (but actually doing everything) in this manner, you lose the greed, you gain freedom. You have nothing to lose but your chains. You have a whole world to win.

NOTES

6. Cyril Birch, ed. *Anthology of Chinese Literature*, trans. Burton Watson (New York: Grove Press, 1965), 121.

21 Beauty

Mao Qiang and Li Ji were beautiful in the eyes of men, but
when the fish saw them, they sank deep. When the birds saw
them, they flew high, and when deer saw them, they dashed
away. Who among them can see real beauty in the world?

—*Zhuangzi*

Philosophers and thinkers all over the world have talked
about beauty for thousands of years. Beauty has become a
sphinx; we think that if we can resolve the meaning of beauty,
we can save our spiritual world. For a Chinese peasant in times
of drought, a black cloud over the land is the most beautiful
thing in the world. A medieval knight might say that a lock of
his lady's hair is the most beautiful thing in the world. A Wall
Street trader may see a rise in the NASDAQ as the most beautiful thing in the world. A mathematician sees beauty in a perfect equation or an elegant proof. In reality, these people are
not talking of beauty but of their need for satisfaction. Beauty
is not a need, not a thirsty lip or an outstretched hand, but
a spiritual experience, a burning heart and a hungry mind.
Beauty is not the achievement of a goal.

When he was in Qi, Confucius heard the music of Shao, and he was so moved that for three months, he didn't taste meat. He said, "I did not imagine that any music existed which could reach such perfection as this."

—*Confucius,* Analects

Confucius experienced real beauty. He did not have an intimate need for this music, his survival did not depend on it, but he could not deny that he had a thirsty heart, humiliated and hurt by the world. When he observed this music, it overcame his need for meals. Beauty is nature. Emerson once said, "A nobler want of man is served by nature, namely, the love of beauty."

As an opposite, success meets our needs. From success, you get lots of things, but not that great, inner feeling that beauty brings us. Beauty is a process without a goal. Beauty is Wu Wei, because it cannot be possessed.

You will not be able to have everything in the world. If you did, where would you put it? You cannot have all the success in the world. If you did, how could you bear it? However, you can have the most beautiful thing in the world, because you do not possess it, and you do not move it into your property from somewhere else. You see it, you experience it, and you feel it, but you do not keep it to yourself. The beauty of beauty is that it is not yours; you cannot take beauty from the universe and deny other peoples' access to it. Success is limited, but beauty is limitless.

Lao Tzu said, "When all under heaven know beauty as beauty, there is then ugliness." (*The Tao Te Ching,* Chapter 2)

The high and nonpossessive beauty.

When people see beauty, they try to possess it. The struggle for beauty has become an ugly nightmare. Only if you do nothing, and let beauty observe you, soak you, and bring you to a world beyond yourself, have you found real beauty.

Those who believe in nature—bred under the starry sky, their minds cultivated by its vastness—will not lose the inspiration during the day in the sound of cities or the fury of crowds. Amidst the disturbances of daily life—the chaos of war, the anarchy of revolution, the death of relatives, with all the accompanying pain and suffering—the starry sky will talk to you, telling you ancient stories, comforting your mind, and soothing your pains. It will say, "Everything is temporary." Again, the Milky Way glimmers, the nightingale sings, the meteors fall, the moon shines, and the stars twinkle. The night grows quiet from the day's noise, and all action takes a rest. The tide rises up and becomes low again. The high wind passes, and the sea becomes calm again. The moonlight shines on the calm water. Waves ripple in the shadows of the willow. It is the way of nature to return to its stillness. With these scenes, the spells of calmness, the keys of strength, are put into our hands. We will forget our temporary worries, because a voice from far away will whisper, "These will also pass."

Beauty is eternally viewing itself in the mirror of the universe. As long as you become a part of the mirror, you will be a part of beauty. You will walk in a garden ever in bloom, but you do not pick the flowers. You fly with a flock of angels without ever fighting with them. You dance with a dragon without slaying it.

Beauty is freedom: freedom from world affairs, from the consequences of efforts and success. When given the choice between success and beauty, Zhuangzi chose beauty.

Zhuangzi was fishing at the River Pu. The king of Chu sent two ministers to tell him that he intended to give him his entire kingdom. Zhuangzi did not put down his fishing pole. He did not even turn his head. "I heard that in Chu there is a divine tortoise that has been dead for three thousand years. The king put it in a box and set it on the shrine to his ancestors. Would the tortoise rather be dead, having its bones worshipped, or alive, dragging its tail in the mud?" The ministers answered, "It would rather be alive dragging its tail in the mud." Zhuangzi said, "Then go away and let me drag my tail in the mud!"

In 1976, I experienced one of the greatest natural disasters in human history. An unprecedentedly strong earthquake shook the Tangshan area, very close to where I attended school. This earthquake killed 260,000 people—more casualties than any earthquake ever recorded. During the night, we felt the whole world was shaking. It was like we were sitting in a boat, tossed up and down in the ocean. We raced from our dorm like mad, and all the students stood on the central sports grounds. We stayed outside for many days without being able to enter the building. A few days later, a strong aftershock came and moved our tall dorms and all the classroom buildings like weeds in the wind. We all stood, watching nature reveal its power.

A classmate of mine named Yuan suddenly said, "That's beautiful." Everybody was quiet. Nobody punched her in the nose, nobody called her a counterrevolutionary, and nobody even called her cynical. Everyone was lost in deep thought.

Her words haunted me for many years, especially when I heard that she committed suicide ten years later. What beauty had she seen in this disaster? This was our building, this was our campus, this was our dorm. That evening, we would have nowhere to sleep, no classroom to go to. How could that be beautiful?

Maybe what she saw was nature revealing its power. Maybe what she saw was that our daily life, which we take for granted, could be torn to shreds. Maybe she saw death. Maybe she saw the figure of human logic against natural disaster. Maybe, for her, beauty had no consequences; it was detached from daily interests, isolated in an unknown world.

My classmate Yuan might have agreed with Zhuangzi, in that there is also beauty in the destructive work of the creator. Master Si, Master Yu, Master Li, and Master Lai were talking to each other: "We'll be friends to those who can take nothingness as the head, life as the spine, and death as the rump." The four people looked at each other and smiled. They agreed with each other in their hearts, so they became friends.

Sometime later, Master Yu got sick, and Master Si went to see how he was doing. "Marvelous!" said the sick man. "The creator has squeezed me into such a shape. My eyes, nose, and mouth are facing up, my back is bent double, my cheek touches my navel, my shoulders are higher than my head, and my neck bones point to the sky. Yin and Yang are all awry. But my heart is at ease, and when I go to the well and look at myself, I say, 'Wow! What a shape the creator has squeezed me into!'"

Four friends who agree with each other in their hearts.

Master Si said, "Are you disgusted?"

"Disgusted? What should I be disgusted with? If my left arm becomes a rooster, I'll crow to greet the dawn. If my right arm becomes a slingshot, I can use it to shoot owls. If my buttocks become wheels, my spirit will ride them. Then I won't need to harness another team of horses. When the opportunity comes, you gain; when the opportunity is gone, you lose. Follow the opportunity, and sadness and happiness will not disturb you. This is what ancient people called 'untying the knot.' If you cannot untie the knot, things will tie you up, and things never beat heaven. Why should I be disgusted?"

Later, Master Lai got sick and was dying. His wife and children surrounded him, crying. Master Li went to visit him and told the wife and children, "Go away. Do not bother him." He leaned on the door and said to Master Lai, "Great is the creator. What will it do for you next? Where will it send you? Maybe it will make you into a mouse's liver or an insect's arm."

Master Lai said, "When parents tell their children to go north, south, east, or west, the children obey. When Yin and Yang give orders to human beings, they should obey too. If I was ordered to die, and I refused to do so, I would be disobedient. There is nothing wrong with the order-giver; the universe carried my body, made me work all my life, nurtured me to old age, and is about to send me to death. That which can give me my life can also give me my death. Suppose a blacksmith was hammering iron, and the iron jumped up and spoke with a human voice: 'I want to be the best sword in the world!' The blacksmith would be shocked. If a human being yells, 'I want to be a man again!' the creator would also be shocked. Now heaven and earth are a big furnace, and the creator is a blacksmith; it can do whatever it wishes."

My classmate Yuan's voice sank into our silences like a dim light that quivers in fear of the shadow. In normal situations, she would be condemned for antisocialist gloating. Yet during that moment in front of that scene, everybody was shocked into silence. She had seen nature distort itself, just as Zhuangzi saw nature turn healthy people into cripples. She was not a philosopher, but her mind rubbed against Zhuangzi's mind, and the sparks flew across the space of 2,500 years.

Here, beauty was doing everything. Nature has the power to do everything. It can build a universe and destroy it. It can transform the order we take for granted into nonexistence. When we see this doing everything, we see that our part is to do nothing. When we see the contrast between doing everything and doing nothing, we have a catharsis. Our anxiety, anticipation, and regret all turn out to be futile. The contrast between doing everything and doing nothing is beautiful.

The real beauty is the beauty that we do not understand. Artists create beauty in color, lines, and shapes. They point out what we see but do not understand in forms that cannot be expressed in words. In traditional Chinese painting, you can always see a high mountain shrouded in mist and a zigzag stream with an idle fisherman. Nature is huge, and the human is small. These paintings also often present images of snow, pavilions, streams, and mountains. Snow, instead of representing bitter winter, symbolizes the coming of the spring. A Chinese saying goes, "Timely snow promises a bumper harvest."

A pavilion is a retreat, a place to rest and appreciate the scenery. The pavilion is a window, opened wide, connecting the heart and the universe. The stream is water, and in Taoism, water is the highest good.

As for the mountains, Confucius said, "The benevolent love mountains. The wise love waters." The mountain symbolizes our solid humanitarian base. When stream and mountain combine, Taoism and Confucianism merge to create harmony. Wang Wei, a Tang dynasty poet, gives the following description: "Fresh rain has fallen on the vacant mountains; autumn's evening approaches. The bright moon is shining through the

An ever-present image in traditional Chinese paintings:
high mountains.

pines, the clear stream flowing over the stones." All the images present a calm, hopeful, and harmonious mood, as if to say to us, "Time changes, water flows, and mountains stay calm. Rest a bit here—you deserve it. The future will be all right. Do nothing now."

In the West, especially in Renaissance art, humans are the center of the picture. In the *Mona Lisa*, the human face occupies most of the canvas. Nature, if it exists, is pushed into the corner. For Westerners, beauty is in humans revealing themselves through the face and the body. When the human body is tested with pain, it can be even more beautiful. Jesus Christ, for example, is tortured on the crucifix. Beyond its symbolic meaning, this is a beauty of mind at its climax. Jesus sacrifices himself with his unspoken suffering, but his face and body keep the beauty of unselfishness and hope. His hope can spread among us, as if we, the human, the center of the world, could defeat any evils, slay any dragons, and recover from our sickness.

This image of human suffering contrasts sharply with traditional Chinese paintings, which usually focus on landscapes. The two different focuses—on nature and humans—show two different approaches to life. The Chinese invented gunpowder to make firecrackers; the Europeans used it to make weapons. The Industrial Revolution started the human process of conquering nature, which is against the Taoist principle of leaving nature alone. Now we are eating the bitter fruits of pollution. Conquering nature and accepting nature contrast but also complement each other. We cannot say which is better; we need both. We should walk on two legs.

We should understand and appreciate nature, but we can also change it. *Do nothing* and *do everything* can be two basic tunes of the song we sing in our universe.

This is the world. We should live in it happily forever, like princes and princesses in fairytales. Someday the world will distort the harmony we take for granted. Yet this distortion can be equally beautiful, so long as we realize that we do not play the role of gods, so long as we do not try to make the world into what we wish it to be. This is art. Only when we realize that we are part of the universe, instead of vice versa, can we say to life calmly and firmly, "I have confidence in you. Go ahead and do what you have to do." In the end, life has its own way of responding to your wishes.

22 Love

Suppose a man loves a woman. When he marries her, there is a 50 percent chance of divorce and a 99.9 percent chance that one spouse will die before the other. The surviving spouse's sadness will be equal to the happiness they had. This does not mean that the couple should not have been married and that they should not have enjoyed the journey of their time together. However, they should realize that their present happiness will someday be lost.

Listen to the story of Duke Ye, told by Liu Xiang of the Han Dynasty:

> Duke Ye loved dragons. He decorated his house with everything and anything dragon: the curtains were embroidered with dragon patterns, the pillars had dragons carved into them. The real dragon in heaven was touched by his affection and decided to pay Duke Ye a visit. He descended to the duke's house. His tail coiled around the backyard, and he stuck his head in the window. When Duke Ye saw the real dragon, he was scared out of his mind by the dragon's size and power. He ran out of his house in great confusion and was not heard from again.

When love peeps in, Duke Ye runs away.

Wealth, marriage, and status can be the real dragon. When we have them, they are not what we imagined. We can still work toward them and be successful just for the fun of it, not for the essence we have imagined. We often fail to understand the relationship between cause and effect. The effect is often against our original intention, and the goal is not always reached. The reason we act is for the bliss of the intention and the beauty of the process. The intention is nobler than the result; the process is more beautiful than the goal. As long as we follow nature, we can do nothing and do everything. Anxiety comes from our self-assigned roles as "god." It is as hard to control our own fortune as it is to control the motion of the universe. Love is attachment; wisdom is detachment. I believe there is plenty of room to maneuver between the two, just as there is between doing everything and doing nothing.

"Rapunzel, Rapunzel, let down your hair." This time, Rapunzel
sends her hair *up* to the dragon. Unlike Duke Ye, she is not afraid
of the real dragon.

To love is to risk not being loved in return, because love
is not a trade. To hope and dream is to risk disappointment,
because the dream and the nightmare are twin sisters. As Lao
Tzu advocated, the two opposite parts should combine and
support each other. Risk is necessary, because the greatest risk
in life is to risk nothing. By clinging to our so-called security,
we are denying life.

Everybody loves love, but can they really handle it? Many
lovers are like Duke Ye, because they love the illusion of love,
not love itself. Love is one of the most beautiful emotions
humans can have. Love is two souls joined together to support each other through sorrow, to strengthen each other in
difficulties, to share with each other in gladness, to merge into

each other in silent memories. Love is not doing; it is being there. Love says to the loved, "Dear one, I'm here to support you, to strengthen you, to share with you, to merge with you." If you love someone, you want the one you love to be there when you feel happy, or when you see the most beautiful sunset. If your heart can really say, "I wish you were here with me," you know you love this person, because you want to share the moment with him or her, to be there with him or her. The essence of love is silence or Wu Wei.

If you love someone, let them go.

The worst line for love is, "You are mine." This is the destroyer of love; the act of owning someone is the opposite of the nonaction of love. In many romantic songs, people compare their lover to the sun or stars. You admire the beauty of the sun and stars, but you do not want to, and cannot, own them. This is the beauty of nonaction, and it should be the beauty of love.

The worst proverb for love is, "All is fair in love and war." War is Wu Bu Wei, doing everything, to conquer your enemies. When love follows the example of war, sound and fury overwhelms serenity and beauty. Conquest and submission become the name of the game. No wonder love and death are the eternal themes of romantic literature.

When possession gets in the way, a happy homecoming becomes a miserable reunion for warriors, their wives, and their dogs. Only the couple who does not believe they own each other can find happiness.

The Intercourse between Yin and Yang

Yin and yang are the basic Taoist dialectical approaches, which can refer to all opposites from negative and positive, back and front, and good and evil. However, the original meaning of yin and yang is female and male. The intercourse of these two opposites is the origin of life.

What is the opposite of death? Many people would say life. Yet in order to continue life from generation to generation, human beings must have sex. Therefore, the opposite of death can be sex. Death pronounces the end of an individual, while sex ensures the continuity of the community. If we understand the tremendous fear of death, we can understand the magnificent attraction to sex. Shining and dark, puzzling and clear, reassuring and dangerous, sex draws poets, dragon slayers, and commoners to climb to the unknown climax, where the two adventurers join together to create a two-person world. They announce their independence and freedom from the world, at least for the moment. The couple has become the god and goddess on Olympus. They have stopped time, eliminated space, and denounced death.

Philosophers, prophets, and gurus have competed to explain this unique phenomenon. Some of them try to oppress the intercourse between yin and yang, while others see it as a form of liberation. Most of them approach it from political or moral perspectives. In China, Confucian puritanism made sex a taboo topic, although hypocritically, traditional Chinese society allowed concubines. Confucius said, "It is hardest to deal with women and petty men. If you are too close to them, they lose their humility. If you keep a distance from them, they resent it." For Confucianists as well as Christians, sex has been seen as a necessary evil that is practiced by unequal partners. Art and literature dealing with sexual relationships was often banned, suppressing the celebration of yin and yang.

Contrarily, Taoists view sex as an action that follows the course of nature and allows for the equal combination of yin (female) and yang (male). For them sex is a topic of health, but not politics; a topic of universal harmony, but not a social pact. Lao Tzu said, "Tao gives birth to one, one gives birth to two, two gives birth to three, three gives birth to ten thousand beings. Ten thousand beings carry *yin* on their backs and embrace *yang* in their front, blending these two vital breaths to attain harmony" (Chen, *The Tao Te Ching*, Chapter 42).

Having realized the harmonious and equal combination between yin and yang, Lao Tzu is probably the earliest feminist. He said, "The female always wins the male by stillness, by stillness it is low-lying" (Chen, *The Tao Te Ching*, Chapter 61). For him, women are equal partners to men in their relationships. With figurative and revealing speech, he proclaims that the female can overcome the male by lying low in stillness, based on his argument that the weak will overcome the strong as dripping water wears holes in stone. Together, man like rock and woman like water create harmony, pleasure, and health. Lao Tzu reached this conclusion not only from his observation of society, but also from his understanding of nature. In nature, the sky and the earth complement each other; fire and water contrast to each other; and male and female support each other.

Men and women were considered the equivalent of heaven and earth, but they became disconnected from one another. While heaven and earth are eternal, men and women suffer a premature death. Heaven and earth touch each other through rain, snow, and rainbows. Men and women should do the same. Each interaction between yin and yang has significance, like the caress between heaven and the earth. Numerous Taoist texts discuss the varying skills and moods in the bedroom. The male and female should follow the natural course of Wu Bu Wei, and do everything to make their encounter harmonious.

The Tang writer Bai Xingjian (776–826 CE) describes how the male and the female should imitate the harmonious beauty of nature during the four seasons. The private movements inside the chamber mirror the seasonal changes outside the window. In the spring, the husband should be tender and frisky, while the wife should be humble and coy. They mimic the playful spring light outside, while the golden orioles sing beak to beak, and the violet swallows fly wing to wing. In the summer, the male and female retreat into a deep, red bed curtain, giving generously and accepting humbly, like the shadows from the sunshine that dance on the bamboo mattress and the willows that touch the lotus pond. In the fall, the couple feels a nostalgic love, just as the hand-fans are stowed away and the autumn fragrance penetrates the bed curtain. During the winter, the couple seeks shelter in a warm chamber, under a thick, embroidered quilt. The husband creates spring sunshine over the wife's snow-like body, which mirrors the pure snow outside.

This most poetic and lusty description of intercourse between yin and yang is from Bai Xingjian's text "Tiandi Yin Yang Da Jiaohuan Yuefu" ("The Grand Ode to the Intercourse between Heaven and Earth, Yin and Yang").[8] The text was lost for a thousand years (maybe because of its bold comparison between sex and nature in four seasons), until the French explorer Paul Pelliot found it in a secret chamber in the mysterious Dunhuang Desert in 1908. This unique discovery should not be wasted and should be applied to our lives today. Our sexual relations will be more harmonious if we align ourselves with the picturesque scenery in nature and the soul-touching chorus of the universe.

Most people consider sex as private, even shameful and guilty. For them, it should be performed in a secret chamber, under a fallen curtain, because the world does not approve of it. Maybe the human world does not, but the natural world always approves. A human combination echoes the natural intercourse between yin and yang. A moment like this should be accompanied by the tenor arias, *"Nessun dorma!"* "None shall sleep! Even you, O Princess, in your cold bedroom, watch the stars that tremble with love and with hope." Since you can perform Wu

Bu Wei, you can do two things at the same time. You may turn off your light, but watch the twinkling stars. You may listen to the gurgling stream and tremble with love. Raise the curtain and let the moon peep in and cheer for you. Nature is your fan forever. Open your heart to nature, and the natural world will stand up and sing its most triumphant opera. With nature, you and your partner defeat the whole world.

While the intercourse between yin and yang can be fascinating, it can also be dangerous. As Lao Tzu warns us, misery lurks beneath happiness. Zhuangzi discusses the danger that lurks in sex on the bed and food on the table: "If people knew of a dangerous road, where one in ten would be killed, they would warn their family and friends, and gather a lot of people to go to this road. Isn't this knowledgeable? Yet there are more dangerous places—beds and tables. People indulge themselves on both of them. This is a big mistake."

Ji Xiaolan (1724–1805 BCE) told a story in *Yuewei Caotang Biji*, his well-known collection of strange anecdotes. A man stayed in a house in the mountains. One evening, he was sitting in the courtyard when he saw a beautiful woman peeking over the yard's wall. He could only see her alluring face. It seemed that she was smiling and flirting with him. The man fixed his eyes on her pretty face. Suddenly, he heard some children crying outside, "A huge snake is coiled around a tree, and it is putting its head on the wall!" The man suddenly realized that the woman was actually a transformed demon with a beautiful human face and a snake body, and she intended to suck his blood. Had he approached her, his life would have been put at great risk.

This story strives to show the hidden consequences of debauchery, which can ruin a person's health and life. As Zhuangzi points out, there lies great danger in the bed. He was so insightful, especially when we realize that there were no sexually transmitted diseases in China before the sixteenth century. Still, Taoist masters realized the danger behind "matters on the bed." Their reason for abstinence was simply to preserve life energy. Nowadays, we face dangers hundreds of times more serious with the rampant spread of sexually transmitted diseases. HIV/AIDS manifests itself as an unprecedented threat, like a snake-transformed phantom coiling over the globe. Today with HIV/AIDS, the opposing forces of life and death have a chilly meeting, thousands of years after Lao Tzu and Zhuangzi warned us that opposites will finally join.

We should heed Lao Tzu and Zhuangzi's advice: follow the guide of nature, savor the delight, but be aware of the consequences. As in all other aspects of Taoism, Wu Wei and Wu Bu Wei must again come together in perfect harmony, like the intercourse between yin and yang, which will announce the triumph of life and the defeat of death.

NOTES

7. Bai Xingjian, "Tiandi Yin Yang Da Jiaohuan Yuefu" (The Grand Ode to the Intercourse between Heaven and Earth, Yin and Yang), *Daojia Yangshengshu* (Taoist Way of Health and Longevity). Chen Yaoting, ed. (Shanghai: Fudan University Press, 1992), 487-488.

 Ambition

If somebody has an ambition when she is young, she can work hard to realize this ambition. When she achieves her goals, she may realize they are not what she really wants; her ambition can betray her. Since she will die someday, she cannot avoid being separated from her goals. Her efforts are in vain. She is a part of nature, part of society. She can work toward her goals, and the work itself, the whole effort, is a realization of natural or social beauty. She can enjoy this beauty, this sense of success, but she should not think that she owns this success. The success itself is temporary.

When we set a goal, we often rely on what other people tell us. We have an aim in life, but we have never been there. Since it is not our own experience yet, we do not know how pleasant it can be; we must depend on other people's descriptions without context. Our own motivations are inspired by other people's words. We work toward a goal, but when we really achieve it, it may not be what we dreamed. Liezi told a story:

A man was born in Yan, but grew up in Chu. When he was old, he came back to his native place. Passing Jin on the journey home, his fellow traveler fooled him into believing that the city wall was the wall of his home town, and he looked sad. The other traveler told him that one temple was his native temple for the God of land, and he sighed with nostalgia. When the traveler told him that a house was where his parents and grandparents had lived, he began weeping. When he was told that a mound was the tomb of his ancestors, he wailed. The other man roared with laughter and said, "That is the state of Jin, my fellow. I have been joking." The man felt very ashamed. When at last he arrived at Yan and saw the city wall and its temple for the God of land, as well as the actual abode and tombs of his ancestors, he was no longer that sad.[9]

The man from Yan was moved by the tomb that was not his ancestors', but when he sees the real tomb of his own ancestors, he is not that sad. His feelings are controlled by illusions created by other people.

Confucius, who occasionally reveals a subtle appreciation of the Taoist approach, also realizes that we often have ambitions for the future at the cost of the present. The following classical Confucian story shows some Taoist tendency.

Once when Zi Lu, Zeng Xi, Ran Qiu, and Gongxi Hua were seated in attendance with the Master, he said, "You consider me as a somewhat older man than yourselves. Forget for a moment that I am so. At present you are out of office and feel that your merits are not recognized. Now supposing someone were to recognize your merits, what employment would you choose?"

Zi Lu promptly and confidently replied, "Give me a country of a thousand war-chariots, hemmed in by powerful enemies, or even invaded by hostile armies, with drought and famine to boot; in the space of three years, I could endow the people with courage and teach them in what direction right conduct lies."

Our Master smiled at him. "What about you, Qiu?" he said.

Qiu replied, "Give me a domain of 60 to 70 leagues, or 50 to 60 leagues, and in the space of three years, I could bring it about that the common people should lack for nothing. But as to rites and music, I should have to leave that to a real gentleman."

"What about you, Gongxi Hua?"

He answered, "I do not say I could do this; but I should like at any rate to be trained for it. In ceremonies at the Ancestral Temple or at a conference or general gathering of the feudal princes, I should like, clad in the Straight Gown and Emblematic Cap, to play the part of junior assistant."

"Zeng Xi, what about you?"

The notes of the zither he was softly fingering died away. He put it down, rose, and replied, saying, "I fear my words will not be so well chosen as those of the other three."

The Master said, "What harm is there in that? All that matters is that each should name his desire."

Zeng Xi said, "At the end of spring, when the making of the Spring Clothes has been completed, I would like to go with five or six newly-capped youths and six or seven uncapped boys, person the lustration in the river Yi, take the air at the Rain Dance altars, and then go home singing."

The Master heaved a deep sigh and said, "I am with Zeng Xi." [10]

The process is more beautiful than the goal. Many modern girls dream of being a princess, but the more beautiful thing is the process to get there, and not the position itself. Princess Diana was one of the most miserable people in the world, because she reached the goal without the process. The climax of her glory was her marriage. All of her later life was spent paying the price of being a princess without having gone through the process. Most winners of the lottery have lives full of disappointment because they did not have the enjoyment of the process of becoming rich. Wealth is not a bad thing, if it stands at the end of hard work. Remember, the rainbow is more beautiful than the pot of gold at the end of it.

Appreciate, but do not own, the beauty.

The rainbow, colorfully transparent and surrealistically floating, is beyond anyone's reach. Viewers admire it in the crisp air after the rain, and nobody is so silly as to claim to own it. This is the beauty of the rainbow. The ambition of ownership is the destroyer of beauty.

If you want anything to happen, you must start from the very beginning. No matter how ambitious you are, you cannot build a pagoda from above. Eighty percent of all our energy is spent in the wrong direction. Think before you move forward; sometimes direction is more important than hard work. As a Chinese saying goes, "You cannot lower your head and pull a cart."

Zhanguo Ce (*Comments on the Warring States*), a book published more than 2,000 years ago, records the following story:

A man wants to travel to the Chu State in the south, but his driver goes north. A stranger asks him, "What are you doing? You want to go south!"

"But I have a very capable driver," replies the man.

"But the Chu State is in the south."

"But I have a lot of money!"

"You have a lot of money, but the Chu State is still in the south."

"I have a fast horse!"

"Yes, you do, but the Chu State is still in the south."

Here we can see that if the direction is wrong, hard work does not help at all. The driver works harder and the passenger only moves farther from the destination. When the direction is correct, the unforced effort, Wu Wei in this case, will lead the vehicle forward. Wu Wei is not idling but quietly contemplating, musing, and setting a correct direction. The world should realize that a driven worker is not more respectable than a relaxed thinker. Let us leave the thinker alone, maybe she is a direction setter.

According to Lao Tzu, people usually fail when they are

A lonely thinker, a respectable contemplator,
and maybe a direction setter of the world.

on the verge of success. They become overconfident, arrogant, and careless when success is in sight and take the last, but wrong, direction. This is why Wu Wei is important. When you do not know what to do, do nothing and let your mind rest. The mind is more powerful than you know. Take a break and let it work!

Also, remember that the process is more beautiful than the goal. The most dangerous thing is not that you cannot grab the sword. It is that once you have it, you either break it, find that you do not like it, or use it for destruction. The moment you have achieved your goals is the most dangerous time, because you may waste or even abuse the achievements you have worked for years to achieve.

NOTES

8. Liezi, *Liezi*, trans. Liang Xiaopeng and Li Jianguo (Beijing: Zhonghua Book Company, 2005), 81.

9. Adapted from Confucius, *Analects*. trans. Arthur Waley (Hertfordshire: Wordsworth Editions Limited, 1996).

25 Flying

To fly has been a universal human dream since antiquity, and so have mythical flying creatures, like dragons. Belief in them has prevailed all over China for thousands of years and has attained a certain reality through historic, literary, mythological, folkloric, social, psychological, and artistic representations. Hardly any symbols saturate Chinese civilization so thoroughly as those of the dragon. Among its many symbolic meanings, the dragon represents a powerful liberation from the bonds of the world, riding on the wind and reaching the heavens. In the air, across the sky, and above the ocean, it effortlessly soars on the wind and disappears among the clouds.

The Taoist imagination enabled the ideal man to soar like a dragon with elevated and sublime spirits. According to a legend in *Shiji, Records of the Historian*, Confucius once said this of Lao Tzu: "Birds fly, fish swim, animals run. Animals can be caught with traps, fish with nets, and birds with arrows. But then there is the dragon; I do not know how it rides on the wind or how it reaches the heavens. Today I met Lao Tzu. I can say that I have seen the Dragon." Here Confucius refers to the effortless grace of Lao Tzu, who does nothing and leaves nothing undone.

"How many times do I have to tell you, Billy?
There are no such things as dragons!"

A scene from the most universal dream.

Flying

In modern times, humans really can fly. John Gillespie Magee, Jr., was born in Shanghai, China, in 1922 to an English mother and a Scotch-Irish-American father. He dreamed of becoming a pilot and fighting against Nazi Germany, but the United States had not yet entered WWII. As an American citizen, he could not legally fight. He entered flight training in the Royal Canadian Air Force anyway. Within the year, he was sent to England to fight against the German Luftwaffe. John soon rose to the rank of Pilot Officer. On September 3, 1941, he flew a test flight in a newer model of the Spitfire V. As John climbed to a height of 30,000, he was struck with inspiration. Soon after he landed, he wrote a letter to his parents. In the letter, he wrote, "I am enclosing a verse I wrote the other day. It started at 30,000 feet and was finished soon after I landed." On the back of the letter, he jotted down his poem:

High Flight

Oh! I have slipped the surly bonds of Earth
And danced the skies on laughter-silvered wings;
Sunward I've climbed, and joined the tumbling mirth
Of sun-split clouds and done a hundred things
You have not dreamed of—wheeled and soared and swung
High in the sunlit silence. Hov'ring there,
I've chased the shouting wind along and flung
My eager craft through footless halls of air. . . .
Up, up the long, delirious burning blue
I've topped the wind-swept heights with easy grace
Where never lark, or even eagle flew—
And, while with silent, lifting mind I've trod

The high untrespassed sanctity of space,
Put out my hand, and touched the face of God.

Just three months later, on December 11, 1941—only
three days after the United States entered the war—Magee
was killed in a midair crash. A farmer testified that he saw the
Spitfire pilot struggle to push back the canopy. The pilot, the
farmer said, finally stood up to jump from the plane. Magee,
the pilot-poet, was too close to the ground for his parachute to
open and he died immediately. He was 19 years old.

As a young man, John Magee seems to have done everything
that many "have not dreamed of." He flew up, up to the "delirious burning blue...where never lark, or even eagle flew." He
tested the limit of ecstasy. The poet here does everything, but

Slipping the surly bonds of Earth.

he does everything with freedom. He "topped the wind-swept heights with easy grace." Magee did nothing, but he reached the height of heroism by liberating himself in the air. He gracefully reached heaven like a dragon.

To "slip the surly bonds of Earth" has long been the dream of Taoism. According to Zhuangzi, Wu Wei, or "doing nothing," refers to the attitude of the Taoist sage or the "ideal person." He is not literally doing nothing, but he engages in transparent and effortless activity. In an ideal realm, the ideal person acts in nonaction, relaxes and wanders, roams away with no particular goal. He flies like a bird, floats like a cloud, swims like a fish, meanders like a stream, blooms into life like a spring flower, and falls to death like an autumn leaf. Just like John the airman, he flies his craft "through footless halls of air" with silent, lifting mind.

Wu Wei is associated with the spiritual flying quality of the free person who has overcome the daily bonds of the ego and is able to experience the totality of things. Magee was like Zhuangzi's sage. He "danced the skies on laughter-silvered wings" and "touched the face of God." He has done Wu Wei, or doing nothing, and Wu Bu Wei, leaving nothing undone, in a heaven at 30,000 feet.

The first rockets were invented in China. The Chinese invented gunpowder and made firecrackers by stuffing it into bamboo tubes. According to legend, the world's first rocket scientist was Wan Hu, a Chinese official of the Ming Dynasty. Five hundred years ago, Wan Hu designed a "flying dragon" by binding two large kites and 47 firecrackers to a chair. He asked 47 torch-bearing assistants to light the firecrackers at the same time. They did so dutifully. A thundering roar and fluttering clouds of smoke followed. The smoke cleared, and Wan Hu was no more.

We do not know whether Wan Hu built his rocket out of a Taoist desire to escape from this world or a Confucian desire to serve his nation by inventing a new mode of transport. I prefer to believe he was a Taoist because of his playful imagination and his burning desire to fly into the great nothingness. Did he fly in one piece into the azure sky? The answer is lost in the smoke of antiquity.

Father, are you sure this is the only way to escape from this world?

In Taoism, flying can be reached by imagination. A soaring mind can also lift us from the binding earth. Zhuangzi told a story of a man named Tian Gen, who once asked Wu Ming Ren (Nameless Man) how to rule the world. Wu Ming Ren reproached him for disturbing his spiritual flying, saying, "Go away, you shallow man! Why do you ask such a vulgar question? I was in the company of the creator. When I get bored, I'll ride on the bird of purity and emptiness, and fly beyond the six ends of the earth, and travel in the realm of nothingness."

"Students, do not look at her. The Witch of the West belongs to another realm. We have our own Taoist way to fly."

Do Nothing in this World

Not everybody experiences ecstasy in midair like John Gillespie Magee, but everybody has the same guaranteed ending—death. Should we be afraid of death, that "undiscovered country?" For several thousand years, sages and philosophers have been exploring what we do "over there." Here, an anonymous person knows what we do there—nothing, and she yearns for it:

On a Tired Housewife

Here lies a poor woman who was always tired,
She lived in a house where help wasn't hired:
Her last words on earth were: "Dear friends, I am going
To where there's no cooking, or washing, or sewing,
For everything there is exact to my wishes,
For where they do not eat, there's no washing of dishes.
I'll be where loud anthems will always be ringing,
But having no voice I'll be quit of the singing.
Do not mourn for me now, do not mourn for me never,
I am going to do nothing forever and ever."

—Anonymous

This tired housewife has a great sense of humor, but at the same time, she is profoundly sad. She cooked, washed, and sewed all her life without any help. Now she yearns for a world where she will do nothing forever. All worries and chores will be gone. She has been too tired, unrewarded, and unappreciated. She begs her friends not to mourn for her. Instead, they should give a standing ovation to the departure of this tired housewife. Lord Byron said, "Sweet is revenge—especially to women." The tired woman delivered revenge to the world, which required her to do everything by telling the world that she is happy to be dead and doing nothing in the other world.

Life usually lasts less than a hundred years, but death is eternal. No wonder it can seem so much more serene, more real, even more interesting than life. Death started before life and will last after life. We can achieve the serenity of this infinite world by letting life take its natural course. The world is won by those who let it go. Life is won by those who dare liberate themselves to join the universe and follow the philosophy of Wu Wei in life. The tired housewife does not need to die to find the peace she wants. This can be done in this life instead of waiting for the next world. The sky would not fall if she took it easy.

Wu Wei is a behavior that arises from a sense of oneself as connected to the world. It is not built by a sense of separateness, but rather by the spontaneous and effortless art of living, which a pilot or a housewife can both achieve. Through understanding this principle and applying it to daily living, from doing tiring chores to dancing in the skies on laughter-silvered wings, we may consciously become a part of life's flow. Nondoing is not passivity, inertia, or laziness. Rather, it is the experience of floating with the wind or swimming with the current.

The principle of Wu Wei carries certain requirements. Primary among these is to consciously experience ourselves as part of the unity of life. Lao Tzu and Zhuangzi tell us to be quiet and vigilant, learning to listen to both our own inner voices and the voices of nature. In this way we heed more than just our mind to gather and assess information. We develop and trust our intuition as our connection to the Tao. We rely on the intelligence of our whole body, not only our brain. All of this allows us to respond readily to the beauty of the environment, which of course includes ourselves. Nonaction functions in a manner to promote harmony and balance. In a sense, the housewife's tiresome life can be as pleasant as Magee's glide over the cloud. She did not have to wait until the next world. She can do nothing and everything in this world.

27 Walking

When I first came to Carleton College, I took a walk with no destination in mind on Bell Field, a sunken soccer field. I circled and circled, as many Chinese people will do for a walk. Two students were sitting on the hill nearby, watching me. Finally, they came to me and kindly asked, "Did you lose something?" From their bemused expressions, I read another, unasked question: "Are you crazy?"

"Thank you," I said. "I'm just walking."

As a matter of fact, English does not have a good equivalent for the Chinese word *sanbu*, loose or scattered steps. I realized later that in the English language, you *walk* with a goal. Walking in a circle without a destination or purpose seems crazy and like a waste of time. Yet walking without a goal is the best healing practice for your mind, your body, and your soul. You are imitating the basic movement of the universe: a moon circling a planet, a planet circling a sun. One-way walking is normal on earth, something unique for "earth animals," but it is abnormal in the universe. If we move like the universe, we do as Einstein said: "It is still the best to concern yourself with eternals, for from them alone flows the spirit that can restore peace and serenity to the world of humans."

"Sir, can we offer you directions?"

Lao Tzu said, "Good running leaves no tracks." (Chen, *The Tao Te Ching*, Chapter 27) The skilled walker just floats through the air without physical or mental tracks. I believe that if you walk with anxiety, with mental knots, you leave invisible tracks of contagious anxiety behind you, infecting anyone who comes across them. Unfortunately, the world is full of tracks of troubled minds, like a freeway during rush hour clogged with harried drivers.

We do a lot of things while walking—too many. We have a goal, a target, or an errand for the walking. We pay too much attention to the goal, too little to the process—and what a pleasant and graceful process it is! We do not allow ourselves to pause, to smell the fresh air, to look at the blue sky, or to restore peace in ourselves. As a matter of fact, we cannot walk, we can only go—go *somewhere*: go shopping, go to work, or go on an errand. Nevertheless, we should relearn how to walk going *nowhere*. I call this "meditative walking." When you practice meditative walking, each step calls you back to the present moment. Each step enables you to connect to the eternal and to create a link between your mind and your body.

Meditative walking brings you to the present, undoing knots in your heart, transforming negative energies to positive. It seems that you are not going anywhere, but you are going here and now. You are engaging in a process without a goal, a doing without achieving. This is walking without going.

Swimming without a goal is beautiful and graceful, almost like flying. Lao Tzu said,

A person with superior goodness is like water,
Water is good in benefiting all beings,
Without contending with any.
Situated in places shunned by many others,
Thereby it is near Tao.
(Chen, *The Tao Te Ching,* Chapter 8)

When you swim, you are closest to the Tao; you are a king reigning over the vast territory of water, which includes the water outside of you and the water inside of you. The practice of swimming meditation unites you with the water outside in order to restore peace and harmony. Do not count laps, do not count time, and do not worry if people stare at you like you are crazy. You are establishing peace in yourself in the territory of water to which you belong.

Doing nothing not only helps you to be serene and healthy, it can also help you "win," a word Taoism can playfully accept. The eagle's flight is a perfect combination of movement and stillness. If we know how to relax in strenuous actions, we can move ahead, like a cloud floating over the mountains, like a river flowing into the ocean, and like a wild swan flying to the horizon.

In college, I was a champion of short-distance running. With 11.2 seconds, I won first prize in the 100-meter race and broke the record of my college. My secret was doing nothing while doing everything. For self-training, I read all available books on short-distance running. I was impressed by an author who wrote that you should relax your body after you begin. The runner should set off at a blistering pace; then they should relax the body, especially the neck and shoulders, for a few steps and take advantage of the momentum. Here, I found the secret of winning. I learned to give myself a few relaxed "centiseconds" during the tense 11 seconds. After setting off, I even yelled to myself *fangsong* (relax), and I let the dash become a float. During these 11 seconds, the wind screamed by my ears, the destination was in view, and my competitors were moving back, while I was trying my best to relax. When my friends congratulated me on my championship, I would say in a humble Chinese way, "I did nothing."

28 Tai Chi Boxing, Doing Nothing

Tai Chi Chuan (Quan), or Tai Chi Boxing or Shadow Boxing, is a Chinese martial art that combines self-defense with healing meditation and breath control. The word *chuan* (Quan) means "fist," emphasizing the lack of weapons or tools in this martial art. Tai Chi Boxing is the most common form of Tai Chi. It is practiced by millions of people for its health benefits, stress relief, and relaxation. The slow, low, and weak flowing movements stimulate the flow of energy, *chi* or *qi*, in the body for health and longevity. By practicing Tai Chi, one's body and mind become integrated. Many people enter a state of Wu Wei. Tai Chi is translated as the "utmost pole," the extreme, the end of the limit. The Tao is beyond the utmost pole. When you reach the end of the limit, you return.

The symbol of Tai Chi is the yin-yang.

The symbol of Tai Chi is the circle of yin and yang, black and white intertwined with each other. In this 5,000-year-old mystifying circle, we do not have a beginning, and we do not have an end. We do not have definition. We do not have a purpose. We do not display.

we are joining the universe
Tai chi's uniform motion =

With Tai Chi's uniform motion, we are joining the universe.
"A journey of a thousand miles must begin with the first step."
(Chen, *The Tao Te Ching*, Chapter 64)

Tai Chi's motion is Wu Wei, doing nothing, because when we do Tai Chi, we move with uniform motion. Uniform motion, according to Newton's laws, is the same as rest. Newton's first law of motion, also called the Law of Inertia, states that an object continues in its state of rest or uniform motion unless compelled to change that state by an external force. In our daily environment on the earth, objects slow down because they are compelled to change speed by a friction force. In Tai Chi, there is no friction, no resistance. We continue with uniform motion.

When we have uniform motion, it is the same as resting; we have become stars and planets of nonaction.

Learning the basic forms does not mean that you *know* Tai Chi. There is always something to improve; think of this as a beginning to a lifelong journey. Knowing the forms is just the beginning.

Attitude in Tai Chi is very important. Do not let your mind wander; feel your place in the universe. Keep in mind these things:

- In order to truly master Tai Chi Boxing, you must be able to assume the correct body positions and be able to control them.

- Your torso should be upright and perpendicular to the ground. Do not lean forward or backward unless the movement calls for it.

- Your legs should be bent, and you should be low most of the time.

- The arms should stretch outwards, not collapse inwards.

- There should be the form of an empty vessel between your bowed legs and outreaching arms.

- Your transitions must be fluid. Think of the transition as part of the movement. Most importantly, speed must be held constant. Think of the earth rotating in space. Should terrorists be able to speed up or slow down the rotation of the earth, our entire world would cease to exist. The earth moves and yet it does not move. It moves with uniform speed, so it does not move. Your Tai Chi Boxing should strive to do the same thing.

- Be flexible! Flexibility is life; stiffness is death. The tongue is flexible, and the teeth are stiff. Which will fall out first?

- The body should expand. Anxiety makes people shrink and protect themselves from the outside world, but to gain awareness of nature, we should relax and expand.

Tai Chi is not a performance. Performance sacrifices the correct way for the entertaining way. Whenever you perform, since your childhood, you have known you have an audience. When you have an audience, you have to show yourself. When you show yourself, you have to be normal. When you are normal, you do things at a normal speed. If you do things slowly, people will think you are not normal, and you are concerned with what other people think. When you do Tai Chi, you should not be concerned with what other people think. You should relax and build a network with the universe. When you build this network, you are spontaneous. Now you do Wu Wei.

People may think you are strange, since they have not seen a human move like this. In the universe, most celestial bodies move in constant motion, in movements with an even speed. We human beings and other animals on the earth act in sporadic motions—very abnormal from the universal point of view. When doing Tai Chi, we move with an even speed, an imitation of the *real* normal motion of the universe. If others think you are strange, you are performing Tai Chi well.

If you have a dog, perform Tai Chi in front of it. The first time you do it, the dog just barks. It will get annoyed, because dogs do not like abnormal movements. You are not performing well in its eyes, so your dog does not know what to do! Do not worry about your dog, and do not worry about other people. They are both bound to the earth. Tai Chi is not a performance but a return to the natural and universal.

Usually, we change our mindset, and our body language follows. In Tai Chi, we change our bodies, and our minds follow. Grace will follow with the right mindset. When our bodies move like a planet, so will our minds.

In my class, I created an imaginary student whose name was Jenny. Smart and individualistic, she would sometimes challenge my teaching, find the contradictions in my lectures, or over-perform what she had learned. This imagined Jenny became a class joke. Students would start laughing as soon as I said, "Jenny, stop doing that, in Tai Chi 101, we can only float five inches above the ground. How many times does our teacher have to tell you that our motto, opposite to that of the Olympics' Faster, Higher, Stronger, is Slower, Lower, and Weaker?"

We should be slower in Tai Chi, because stillness is the essence of the universe. The earth circles the sun, the moon

"Jenny, how many times does the teacher have to tell you that we
can only float five inches above the ground?"

circles the earth, but we cannot even feel the movement. By
being still, we can be closer to the essence of the universe.

We should be lower in Tai Chi, because by being low, we
come closer to the earth.

We should be weaker, because Tai Chi is not for fighting; it
is for peace. Humans used to need strength to survive, attack,
and kill. In the beginning, Tai Chi was used for fighting, and
we can still see this history in its movements; but it has lost
its martial emphasis. Now we advocate the weak as Lao Tzu
would, and we use our strength to heal, not to wound. We
should be slow, low, and weak—like water. Lao Tzu said:

Low, slow, and weak, Tai Chi brings us back to Nature.

Nothing under heaven
Is softer and weaker than water,
Yet nothing can compare with it
In attacking the hard and strong.
Nothing can change place with it.
That the weak overcomes the strong,
And the soft overcomes the hard,
No one under heaven does not know,
Though none can put it into practice.
Therefore a sage said:
"One who receives the filth of a state
Is called the Master of the Altar of the Soil and Grain;

One who shoulders the evils of a state
Becomes the king under heaven."
Straightforward words appear to be their reverse.
(Chen, *The Tao Te Ching*, Chapter 78)

29 Tai Chi Sword, Doing Everything

Tai Chi can be performed with a sword, but we do not want to fight with our swords. We want to play with the clouds and the mountains! Tai Chi Sword is as peaceful as the movement of Tai Chi Boxing, but the illustrative and the dramatic movement of Tai Chi Sword brings the art of Tai Chi to a new peak. The sword is the king of Chinese short-range weapons. It can be deadly in combat. A sword fight requires a level of violence and a mental alertness that not many peace-loving people would want to have; but paradoxically, this practice aims at self-cultivation, longevity, and peace. As Lao Tzu says, "Everything goes toward the opposite extreme."

A hole in the end of the sword's hilt is used to attach a long, red tassel that balances the double-edged blade, thus forming a combination of yin and yang. Despite the threatening sword, Tai Chi Sword has more elegant, dramatic, dance-like characteristics. In contrast to the uniform speed of Tai Chi Boxing, Tai Chi Sword allows acceleration and pause during the continuity of a performance. The points of the sword move from various directions with surprises and variety. If we say Tai Chi Boxing is peacefully doing nothing, Tai Chi Sword is more dramatically doing everything.

The imaginary student Jenny would say, "Wait a minute! Last week, you told us to go rambling without a destination in Tai Chi. Now you are telling us to have a target in mind with Tai Chi Sword. Which side are we going to settle on?"

Jenny wants to find out if she should do nothing or everything with Tai Chi Sword.

Zhuangzi said, "It is different to drift with the Tao; there is neither praise nor blame. Sometimes you're a dragon, sometimes you're a snake, floating with time, never focusing on one thing, up and down, using harmony as measurement."

My answer to Jenny is this: You, disciples, settle between aim and aimlessness, between being good for something and being good for nothing, between Wu Wei and Wu Bu Wei. Basically, Tai Chi Sword is the same as Tai Chi Boxing in that it brings the mind and the body into harmony. The sword helps the performer make an extension of his body. It is essential to enlarge the mind through the tip of the sword. Energy travels from the earth to the feet and is guided through the whole body, through the torso, and to the tip of the sword. It is often said by the masters of Tai Chi Sword that the waist, not the arms, moves the blade. Beginners who move the arm, or disconnect the movement between the arm and the whole body, demonstrate a lack of understanding of Tai Chi principles. The whole body should remain in flux. While the sword spins easily in the air, the performer flies. The feet feel as if they are dragged up by the sword three inches above the ground. This flying would lead the performer to the arch of the sky, to touch the face of the Supreme Being, whether that is God or Nature.

The hand that is not holding the sword should be held with the first two fingers extended and the ring finger and pinky curled in, with the thumb over the ring-finger knuckle. Some people call this hand Secret Sword or Sword Amulet. The two pointed fingers actively cooperate with the hand that holds the sword. They point at the direction the sword would go to lead the performer's energy and attention to that direction, or deliberately point to other directions to distract the imagined opponents. Thus, the tip of the sword, the tip of the tassel, and the tips of the fingers form three points in a sphere, circling around the body in different directions and balancing the energy. It can be a most elegant image, when a master stands inside these three points with her flexing body changing from standing on her toes to doing a split on the ground. A new dimension, a new magical field is created.

This is an ode to possibilities, to courage, and to doing everything possible.

Zhuangzi offers an extraordinary passage about the art of
the sword:

The sword of the Son of Heaven... is designed in accord
with the Five Phases, assessed by its punishment and bounty,
drawn by means of the Yin and Yang, wielded in spring and
summer, and strikes its blow in autumn and winter. With this
sword you can

> Thrust and there's nothing ahead,
> Brandish and there's nothing above,
> Press down on the hilt and there's nothing below,
> Whirl it round and there's nothing beyond.

Up above, it breaks through the floating clouds; down
below, it bursts through the bottom of the earth. Use this
sword once, and it will discipline the lords of the states, the
whole empire will submit.

The sword of the prince of a state has clever and brave
knights for its point, clean and honest knights for its edge, worthy and capable knights for its spine, loyal and wise knights for
its hand-guard, dashing and heroic knights for its hilt. With
this sword you will

> Thrust and there's nothing ahead,
> Brandish and there's nothing above,
> Press down on the hilt and there's nothing below,
> Whirl it round and there's nothing beyond.

Use this sword once, and it will be like the quake after a clap of thunder, within the four borders, none will refuse to submit and obey your commands.

The sword of the common man is to have tousled hair bristling at the temples, a tilted cap, stiff chinstrap, coat cut up short at the back, have glaring eyes, be rough of speech, and duel in your presence. Up above, it will chop a neck or slit a throat; down below it will burst lungs or liver. This is the sword of the common man, it is no different than cockfighting. In a single morning, man's fated span is snapped." [11]

We do not fight the natural order of things, nor do we leave our tasks undone. The Common Man will act, but he will act with only his own petty aims in mind. When we carry the Sword of the Son of Heaven, our actions are most effective, because they are done in harmony with the flow of the universe.

Greet people with words, not swords.

I respect you, since you are alive and have a battle to fight every day. But may you stop for a while to smell the flowers between your battles, since you are only here for a short visit. Greet people with words, not swords. Be kind! Everyone you meet on the way has a hard battle to fight.

> The world has no room for cowards. We must all be ready somehow to toil, to suffer, to die. And yours is not the less noble because no drum beats before you when you go out into your daily battlefields, and no crowds shout about your coming when you return from your daily victory or defeat.
>
> —*Robert Louis Stevenson*

不佩剑的武士
生活战场上的英雄
A warrior without sword
A hero in daily battlefields
Qiguang Zhao
赵启光 2006

A warrior without sword, a hero in daily battlefields.

The distinction between Tai Chi Boxing and Tai Chi Sword represents the contrast of doing nothing and doing everything. Tai Chi Boxing flows with whatever may happen and lets your mind be free. This is Wu Wei, or doing nothing. Yielding is the use of the Tao of Tai Chi. Even in small movements, there is grandeur. Do not hurry, do not worry; you are only here for a short visit. You may not be able to accomplish a grand mission today, but stop by and move along with the ten thousand objects of the universe!

For Tai Chi Sword, you stay centered by completing whatever your sword ventures to do. This is doing everything, or Wu Bu Wei, leaving nothing undone. Reversing is the motion of the Tao of Tai Chi Sword. Beautiful things are all around you: the air is close to you, the sky is above you, and you can even lift your head and see the stars. Your sword cannot touch them, but their beauty is there with you. You can amplify the small and flow with the universe.

The Law of the Unity of Opposites is the fundamental law of the universe. Things that oppose each other also complement each other. Thus, Tai Chi Boxing and Tai Chi Sword complement one another like the two sides of a crystal jade.

NOTES

10. Zhuangzi, *The Inner Chapters*, trans. A.C. Graham (Indianapolis: Hackett Publishing Company, Inc., 2001), 246.

30 Happiness

Happiness is internal. It does not depend on what we have but on what we are. It does not depend on what we get but on what we experience. Our hearts are lifted when we behold a rainbow, but we do not want to own it. Most of us do not even want to travel to the end of it to find the pot of gold. We do not have to, because we see the beauty shining against the clouds, and that is happiness enough for us. We do nothing with it except let it shine in our hearts without trying to possess it.

Liu An of the Han Dynasty wrote a story about a lost horse:

An old man who lived on the northern frontier of China was skilled in interpreting events. One day, his horse ran away to the nomads across the border. Everyone tried to console him, but he said, "What makes you so sure this isn't a blessing?"

Some months later, his horse returned, bringing back with her a splendid stallion. Everyone congratulated him, but he said, "What makes you so sure this isn't a disaster?"

Their household was richer by a fine stallion, which the man's son loved to ride. One day he fell from the horse and broke his leg. Everyone tried to console the man, but he said, "What makes you so sure this isn't a blessing?"

A year later the nomads came across the border, and every able-bodied man was drafted into the army. The Chinese frontiersmen lost nine of every ten men. Only because the son was lame did father and son survive to take care of each other.

This story, first told 2,000 years ago, has become a Chinese axiom: "The old man of the frontier lost his horse." It reminds us that blessing turns to disaster and disaster to blessing; the changes have no end, nor can the mystery be fathomed. Our happiness does not depend on what we own. Things like horses and gold come and go. To be happy, one must understand that the gain and loss of material things is simply an ever-changing flow of the river. There are splashes, rises, and falls, but we should remember a simple axiom that exists in all languages: This also will pass.

Lao Tzu said, "Calamities are what blessings depend on, in blessings are latent calamities" (Chen, *The Tao Te Ching*, Chapter 58). The great ocean sends us drifting like a raft, the running river sweeps us along like a boat; but we do not tell the ocean to stop its tides, and we do not tell the river to flow slower. We just join them to celebrate the existence of happiness and freedom. We let water carry our boat to a new adventure. This is why, when we face real ecstasy, we stop doing everything, even holding our breath.

Poetry is the record of the happiest moments of human life. The poet sees the beauty around her, and she wants to put this beauty into a rhythmic pattern that responds to the sight. Poetry is important for all cultures; it has been the center of Chinese civilization for 3,000 years. Chinese officials were poets because of their literary talents, having passed civil examinations on

Rivers flow, boats sail, and the present becomes the past.
This also will pass.

essay and poetry writing. China was a country ruled by poets, many of whom were Taoists—full-time, part-time, real, and pretending Taoists. Observing nature and interpreting life with natural phenomena, they escaped from political, social, and economic pressures.

One of China's most famous Taoist poets, Li Bai (or Li Bo; 701–762 CE) was known for his carefree lifestyle. Most people agree that he is the best Chinese poet because of his unconstrained and joyous understanding of life against the magnificent background of nature. The magic in his poetry comes from his spontaneous enjoyment of life and nature.

Poem 1: Question and Answer in the Mountains

You ask me why I live in the green mountains.
I smile without answering, but with a heart at leisure.
Peach flowers drift away in the stream;
There is another heaven and earth inside the human world...

If no one else comes to your garden party,
invite the moon as your guest.

Poem 2: Drinking Alone Under the Moon

One pot of wine among flowers
Drinking alone without dear ones
Raising the cup and inviting the moon as a guest.
With the shadow, we have a company of three.

The moon cannot take a sip,
The shadow follows me in vain.
For now, I have the moon and the shadow as my companions,
Taking advantage of the spring while it lasts.
When I sing the moon wanders,
When I dance the shadow scatters,
When we are sober, we enjoy each other's company,
When we are drunk, we go our separate ways.
We'll have a cold friendship,
Looking for each other through the clouds in the sky.

Nature is the best company, silent like the bamboo or
clucking like the chicken.

The first poem describes the life of a hermit, an ideal Taoist in Chinese traditional literature. In the mountains, he finds happiness and enjoys himself. "Enjoying oneself" is a wonderful English phrase missing in many languages, including Chinese. Although to "enjoy yourself" means to be happy and enjoy the fun, it literally means finding happiness within yourself. In daily life, many people become burdens on themselves. They need jobs, sports, cards, gambling, and smoking to stay occupied. The Taoists seek a way to enjoy themselves without occupation. They can be alone and be happy by finding company in nature. They are not their own burden.

In the second poem, the greatest Chinese poet is alone and lonely, but in a subtle way, he transforms this loneliness into an ecstasy that merges with the flowers, the moon, and the shadow around him. Using the vocabulary of social life, like "company" and "friendship," he builds a happy trust with nature and liberates himself from the desire to seek happiness from other people. He admires the moon, and he experiences a kind of happiness as cold as the moonlight.

Li Bai reaches freedom in nature. He expresses his ecstasy in poems just like Zhuangzi did in his philosophical stories. They both found their happiness in nature and threw off the shackles of society. They saw dignity and self-respect in the natural world that was only understood by people who shared the same feelings. Li Bai is like the fish described by Zhuangzi:

Zhuangzi and Hui Zi took a walk along the bank of the river. Zhuangzi said, "The fish swim with such ease. They're so happy."

Hui Zi said, "You are not a fish. How do you know they're happy?"

Zhuangzi said, "You are not me. How do you know I do not know the fish are happy?"

Hui Zi said, "I am not you. Of course I do not know if you know. But you are not a fish. You do not know if the fish are happy. So there!"

Zhuangzi said, "Let's go to the root of the matter. You asked me how I know the fish are happy. So you agree that I know they're happy, but you want to find out how I know it? I'm standing here on the bank of the river."

Fish are content because they are doing what they are supposed to do. They swim, bubble, and never dream of being something else. Li Bai with his moon, the horse with its grassland, and the fish with its water all reach the realm of happiness. They do not need other people's approval, so they are not the prisoners of public opinion. Happiness is found within; material pleasure and public admiration come from the outside. The inner happiness always surpasses the superficial enjoyment.

Inner happiness demands a calm and individual environment. This environment liberates us from the anxieties caused by our daily necessities. Anxiety is crucial for survival—but only in quick flashes: It damages one's inner health and society's harmony in the long run. Calmness widens wisdom, expands tolerance, and increases health. Quiet joy strengthens our existence and allows us to make a contribution to the world. When we are frightened, angry, or depressed, we shrink into an invisible shell around us, but at the same time, we project a dark cloud onto others surrounding us. As a Chinese saying goes, "One sad person sitting in the corner makes all the people in the room feel unhappy." In contrast, a happy person spreads the aroma of flowers, the shadows of the rainbow, and the individual calmness to benefit the collective.

A society is composed of individuals, and each individual is responsible for the group status. Philosophers have talked for centuries about altruism—sacrificing oneself for society. While we new Taoists agree with this idea of selflessness, I should add that each individual's mood alone determines the world's collective mindset. It would be very dangerous for an unhappy person to hold power, because he can make the world join his misery. History has proved this again and again. Just like the people in power, each one of us can impact larger humankind. If you make yourself happy and healthy, you will add one happy and healthy grain to the ocean of the world. Sometimes, you feel that you are doing nothing for the human race beyond being happy yourself; as a matter of fact, you are doing everything for its harmony. Your status of cheerful mind will add a colorful band to the multicolored rainbow of the world. This kind of Wu Wei is also a Wu Bu Wei.

Being happy is natural. You will be happy if you let your mind perform Wu Wei. European and American culture is a culture of guilt. People are taught to fear the punishment of an invisible hand. Shrug off the guilt that you have allowed the invisible force to place upon you. You are limitless. There is no happiness that you cannot achieve. Chinese culture is a culture of shame. People are taught to fear losing face. Throw away the shame you have allowed the visible society to place on you. There is no sadness in life that cannot be reversed.

No Regret

Reach the pole of emptiness,
Abide in genuine quietude.
Ten thousand beings flourish together,
I am to contemplate their return.
Now things grow profusely,
Each again returns to its root.
To return to the root is to attain quietude,
It is called to recover life.
(Chen, *The Tao Te Ching,* Chapter 16)

Have no regret; you are not responsible for everything that has happened to the world. You are not responsible for everything that has happened to you and your family. You are a drop of water in the ocean, and your position is decided by the movement of a body trillions of times larger than you. Your best relief is to realize you are not a god. Nobody says that they are a god, but many people believe that they have the ability of God to control everything around them. Therefore, they regret that things do not happen in the way that they would like.

Every night, when you take off your socks, please leave all your problems on the floor with them. Have no fear, your socks will not be lost, and the world will come back to you when you put the socks back on the next morning. Your day is done. You are like a ship drawn to the harbor, like a seagull listening to the evening music of the tide. You are like an autumn leaf falling to the earth, like a homesick child returning home. Be still and be peaceful when you enter the sweet world of doing nothing. You have to leave everything, everybody, and every worry behind you. Lao Tzu said, "Reach the pole of emptiness, abide in genuine quietude. Ten thousand beings flourish together, I am to contemplate their return." (Chen, *The Tao Tê Ching,*, Chapter 16) When you go to sleep, enter the void, join the stillness and quietness.

The most valuable thing is life; we only get one. At death, a person should be able to say, "I am familiar with this, because I have practiced it every night by leaving everything behind me before going to bed. I did something, and I am going to do nothing. I did not have regret all my life, and I do not have it now."

Regret lurks behind your decisions. Your idea may start out like spring flowers ready to bloom. As soon as the decision is made, there is a crash of thunder. Regret comes in like a summer storm, crashing along with rain so thick that the flowers in your mind are drenched. Then there comes a gentle lament, like an autumn drizzle, that whips the surface of your heart, until repentance, like winter snow, floats down and seals your bleeding wounds.

Lao Tzu said, "No action, no regret." Action causes regret, because no single action can be exactly correct the first time. The only way to do nothing wrong is to do nothing. Lao Tzu's "no action, no regret" reflects his theme of Wu Wei. Wu Wei, in this case, is not to avoid decisions in order to avoid regret, but to flow like a river from one correction to another. *Correct,* as an English adjective, means making no mistake. The English word *correct,* as a verb means to change something in order to make it right. Therefore, to be correct, one should continuously correct oneself, instead of bemoaning past mistakes.

This is, as a matter of fact, doing everything. When we walk, we move one foot forward. Soon the direction is wrong, and we have to move it backward. Do we regret that we moved the foot wrongly first time? No. We just constantly change the direction of our two feet, and the whole body moves forward smoothly. Our feet are doing everything (Wu Bu Wei) by moving in opposite directions, and our body is doing nothing (Wu Wei) by moving forward. Therefore, our minds have no regret, because they allow those contradictions to proceed naturally.

Everything will resolve itself sooner or later. This is the way of the Tao. Walk through life without fear for the future or regret for the past. Practice being nothing. In being nothing, you will turn into everything without fear. Watch the clouds in the dawn. As they pass the rays of morning sun, they are tinged but unruffled, penetrated but undisturbed. When they pass the mountains and gorges, they are neither elated by the mountains nor depressed by the ravines. They seem to do nothing but have actually done everything. The clouds will never fear floating toward the peaks ahead, nor will they regret having passed over a valley. This is the mind of Wu Wei and Wu Bu Wei: never elated nor depressed, but rather always flowing at peace.

Watch the way a stream flows effortlessly and passes over the rocks that get in its way. The rocks on the bottom make the limpid water bubble melodiously. Obstacles, like rocks in the stream, can make the path of life more beautiful, so that James Maurice Thompson can say, "Bubble, bubble, flows the stream, like an old tune through a dream." That is the way of life, unencumbered by little impediments. However, the stream takes a bend or diverges around rocks. Water, as Lao Tzu said, "overcomes but never argues, benefits but never claims the benefits." It makes the best of the situation. Overcoming, giving up, doing nothing, and doing everything, the stream bubbles forward without fear or regret. This is what life should be.

Once I asked my father to write something in my notebook. This is what he wrote:

To Qiguang:

Before I turned 80 years old, I used to have a motto: Be strict with yourself and lenient towards others. Now that I am 80 years old, I have a new motto: Be lenient with yourself and lenient towards others. I do not know whether I can correct myself at this age.

Dad, 1997

A very wise man, a professor of physics, and the dean of a well-known university, my father had spent 80 years learning how to treat himself and others: We should treat ourselves with the same forgiving compassion as we give others. Nothing in the world is without flaws, so be tender and kind to others and yourself when you or others stumble. Let us walk our own way, change the direction of our feet, and let others talk. Correct, change, and live without regret, and let the universe follow its own course.

Life and Death

Heaven and earth are long lasting.
The reason why heaven and earth are long lasting:
Because they do not live for self.
Therefore they last long.
Thus the sage puts his body behind,
Yet his body is in front.
He regards his body as external,
Yet his body remains in existence.
Is it not because he is selfless
That he can fulfill himself.
(Chen, *The Tao Te Ching*, Chapter 7)

To achieve longevity, we must join the universe. To join the universe, we must think in reverse. Sometimes the Tao sounds like nonsense, but if we think outside the box, it becomes the greatest sense.

The world is divided into opposites. Everything has two sides that coexist. When one side is denied, it develops into the other side. To go forward, we must go backward; everything requires an opposite. When you walk, one foot moves forward and the other pushes back. It is the back foot that pushes your body forward. In aging, the more you stay behind—acting slowly, staying young—the longer you live. In other words, by staying behind, you get ahead.

This process should be natural, effortless, and not achieved through force. When forms change, they can transform without changing their structure, like clouds or flowers.

> At birth a person is soft and yielding,
> At death hard and unyielding.
> All beings, grass and trees, when alive, are soft and bending,
> When dead they are dry and brittle.
> Therefore the hard and unyielding are companions of death,
> The soft and yielding are companions of life.
> Hence an unyielding army is destroyed.
> An unyielding tree breaks.
> The unyielding and great takes its place below,
> The soft and yielding takes its place above.
> (Chen, *The Tao Te Ching*, Chapter 76)

Lao Tzu's wisdom can be seen in numerous phenomena. Everyone has teeth and a tongue. Which is softer? The tongue, of course. Which falls out first? Of course, the teeth. Have you ever heard of anyone's tongue falling out?

One of Aesop's famous tales, "The Oak and the Reeds," reflects the same concept. A very large oak was uprooted by the wind and thrown across a stream. It fell among some reeds, which it thus addressed: "I wonder how you, who are so light and weak, are not entirely crushed by these strong winds." They replied, "You fight and contend with the wind, and consequently you are destroyed; while we, on the contrary, bend before the least breath of air, and therefore remain unbroken, and escape." We yield and we live. We yield more, and we live longer. However, death will come to us anyway.

Which is more normal, life or death? If life is normal, why have humans not found life anywhere in the universe except the earth? If death is so abnormal, why does the whole starry sky radiate the shining light of nonlife?

If life is normal, why does it belong to you for only 80 or 90 years, while death embraces you for the eternities before your birth and after your death?

The lifeless surface of Mars is normal. Its scenery, waterless and lifeless, is more representative of the universe than the Earth's. The wet surface of the Earth is the anomaly. Life, as far as we know, could not exist without liquid water, which is rare in the universe. No water, and consequently no life, has been found on other planets. Therefore, death is more the essence of the universe. When we die, we just return to normal. We should not cling to the temporary abnormality that is life and refuse the eternal and universal norm.

The person who fears death is like the child who has forgotten the way home. Liezi told a story about Duke Jing of Qi:

Duke Jing climbed up Mount Niu and looked over his capital. He began to cry. "What a magnificent capital! How can I die and leave behind this flourishing town, these verdant forests?"

His two ministers, Shi Kong and Liang Qiuju, also began to weep. "Thanks to Your Highness, we can feed ourselves with our simple food and get around on our humble carriages.

Even though we live only modest lives, we do not want to die! And the thought of our lord dying is unbearable!"

Yangzi stood nearby, laughing into his beard. Duke Jing frowned. Wiping his eyes, he turned to Yangzi. "I am quite sad here, and Shi Kong and Liang Qiuju are weeping with me. Why are you laughing?"

"If a worthy sovereign were to reign forever," said Yangzi, "your grandfather or Duke Huan would still be king. If a brave ruler were to reign forever, Duke Zhuang or Duke Ling would still be our lord. If any of these men were still in power, you would never have succeeded to the throne. Your Majesty might be farming in the fields in a straw coat and bamboo hat, without any time to ponder your death. Reigns have followed reigns until at last your turn came, and you alone lament it. I laugh because I'm looking at an unjust lord and his two yes-men."

Duke Jing was ashamed. He penalized himself with one cup of wine and his attendants with two.

Zhuangzi once told a story:

When Zhuangzi's wife died, Huizi went to console him. He found Zhuangzi sitting cross-legged, drumming on a pot and singing. Huizi said, "You lived with her and she raised your children. Now she is dead. It would be bad enough if you didn't cry. But now you are drumming and singing. Isn't this too much?"

Zhuangzi said, "Definitely not. When she first died, how could I not mourn? Then I realized there was no life in the beginning. Not only no life, but there was no shape. Not only was there no shape, but there was no energy. In the subtle

Should we cry or laugh over the city we will
lose some day because of death?

chaos, changes happened. Energy emerged. Energy became
shape, shape became life, and now life has become death. This
is just the same as the succession of spring, summer, autumn,
and winter. My wife was sleeping calmly in a big hall, and I
followed her wailing and crying. Then I realized that I did
not understand the rules of life. So I stopped crying."

The message of Zhuangzi's story is consistent with that of
numerous Taoist stories: death is a natural return to peace and
eternity. However, if Taoists are so comfortable with this "big
return," why are they so obsessed with longevity and immortality? The Taoist tradition is probably the most famous in the
world for its pursuit of the elixir of life through alchemical

"miracle drugs." If they were not afraid of death, why did they work so hard to avoid it?

You can linger at the top of the mountain and wait for the sun to set, but that does not mean you are afraid of going home to the valley. Taoists love life, but they do not fear death. Their search for immortality comes from a desire to stay a little longer in the lively and familiar realm of life, not from a terror of the unknown and quiet domain of death.

Zhuangzi celebrates his wife's return to Nature.

Which is more interesting, here or there?

We will only be in this world for a short time, but we will be in the other world forever. Death must be interesting, because we have never experienced it; but life is interesting, too, because we have been there, done that. We want to enjoy the adventure as long as possible and do everything before we do nothing.

If life is a dream, let us keep the dream long and sweet. If life is a game, let us make it fun. If life is a one-way journey, let us stop, go outside, and enjoy the scenery. Why hurry? Why always ask, "Are we there yet?" With a healthy understanding of death, we can have a long, healthy, and fearless life.

The barrier between life and death is not absolute. Really, we do not understand death at all. Without knowing anything about it, how do we know that it is not better than life? If we understood death, we would not cry over it. We are not afraid of death; we are afraid of the unknown.

In the Jin dynasty (265–420 CE), when Taoism was not only a theory, but was also practiced by many scholars as a way of life, there was a well-known group called "the Seven Sages of the Bamboo Forest." Among the seven sages, Liu Ling was the one least interested in worldly affairs. According to *History of the Jin Dynasty,* Liu Ling was ugly, free-spirited, quiet, and socially awkward. His spirit soared through the universe and did not distinguish between the ten thousand objects of the world. When he met two other sages of the bamboo forest, Ruan Ji and Ji Kang, the three of them were pleasant and carefree and entered the forest hand in hand.

Liu Ling's instructions: "Bury me where I fall."

According to *Shishuo Xinyu*, a book of historical anecdotes by Liu Qingyi (403–444 CE), Liu Ling often took off his clothes and drank wine at home. When people saw him and laughed, he answered, "I take heaven and earth as my house, my house as my trousers. What are you doing in my trousers?" He did not care about property, and often he rode in a small cart with a bottle of wine, followed by a boy carrying a hoe. His instructions to this boy were, "When I die, bury me where I fall." He paraded around with a boy with a hoe to announce that death is not something to be afraid of, but something as normal as life, perhaps even more normal.

Zhuangzi considers death a natural change of small forms in the infinite universe:

A strong man can carry away our boat no matter how deeply
we hide it in the valley.

The huge clump of earth carries my body, puts me to work all my life, nurses me through old age, and lays me to rest with death. Therefore, the one who can give me life can also give me death. You hide your boat in a valley and your fishing tackle in a marsh, and you think it's safe, but at midnight a strong person can carry them away without your knowing it. It's proper to hide a small thing in a big thing, but you still may lose it. If you hide the world in the world, you will not lose it. This is the universal law. People are happy when they get a body, but the changes of the body are endless; therefore, the happiness is limitless.

When the day comes to die, we are very afraid. We want to own, to cling to, this thing we call life, but it is only one of millions of transformations. Leaves fall, the sun sets, stars burn out, and we die. Life and death are different stages of the same process. Therefore, if you think well of life, you must think well of death.

Before I leave this world, I am never going to say,
"I didn't do this"or "I regret I did that." I am going to say:
"I came, I went, I did nothing, I did all."

Appendix A

When the Red Guards Knock

All incoming Carleton freshmen are given a common reading book to discuss when they arrive at college. In 2003, that book was Balzac and the Little Chinese Seamstress, *and Qiguang Zhao was asked to speak at the opening convocation about the book. The following is an excerpt from that speech, given at Skinner Memorial Chapel at Carleton College on September 11, 2003:*

Archimedes once said, "Give me a lever long enough and a fulcrum on which to place it, and I shall move the world." But where should we place this fulcrum?

Physics tells us that the longer the distance between the two objects, the more powerful the lever. We must build our lever on our connections to the unfamiliar world of nature, beauty, and our fellow humans. On that solid ground, we can move the world.

I am a witness to that power of connection. When I was just about your age, I experienced China's Cultural Revolution. The Cultural Revolution was actually a revolution of anti-culture, which attempted to create a proletarian revolutionary culture by cutting all connections between modern China, traditional China, and the rest of the world.

At the beginning of the Cultural Revolution, the Red Guards searched houses for "bourgeois books and objects." The first group who came to my parents' house was a group of college students. They were students of my parents, who were both professors of physics. One evening, the Red Guards knocked loudly at our front door. At that critical moment, I remembered that my mother had a diary which would have been extremely dangerous if it fell into the hands of the Red Guards. I grabbed the diary, and rushed out our back door just as the Red Guards were entering the front door. I ran for a mile and ducked into a public restroom.

The restroom was quiet. The moon and stars shone through a window overhead; I could hear the familiar lyrical chirpings of the crickets and the unfamiliar militant songs of the marching Red Guards. I looked at the well-kept diary. I wanted to keep it alive in my heart before it sank into oblivion. Under the moonlight, I quickly read my mother's diary, then tore it off page by page and flushed it down the toilet. Most of the diary was written in exquisite Chinese calligraphy. Parts of it were written in English, which I could not read at that time. In two hours, I finished the job and learned for the first time how my mother grew from a remote countryside girl into a professor of physics, a very rare success in her time. In a nation full of wars, famine, and revolution, my mother was motivated to connect herself with the world through the pursuit of knowledge. She had found solid ground to stand on in an unpredictable time.

I left the restroom and looked up at the stars in the night sky. They were tranquil, mysterious, and extremely beautiful, forming a sharp contrast to the dark earth. When I returned home, the Red Guards were gone. My parents' house was a mess, but strangely, though their personal and academic writings had been taken away, most of my parents' thousands of books were untouched. My mother was relieved to learn that her diary was destroyed instead of being taken by the Red Guards.

"They are my students in the physics department," my father said. I did not know whether he was rejoicing over the limited damage or lamenting the violation of a sacred Confucian relationship, that between teacher and students. I only understood his comment many years later, after the Cultural Revolution, when my father became the dean of the University. The first policy he suggested was to require science majors to study humanities and humanities majors to study science. The Red Guards had allowed themselves to be led toward destruction because they lacked comprehensive knowledge of the world and a sense of history. These days, we often talk about good and evil. I believe that evil occurs when ignorance and power meet.

This house search was just the beginning; more groups of Red Guards came in the following few days. The newcomers were mostly high school students. They were more violent and burned nonrevolutionary books. My family's decision was probably unique during the Cultural Revolution: when the Red Guards knocked, we would turn off the lights and not open the door. Group after group of Red Guards passed by our dark windows or pounded on our door but left without breaking in. They were not thorough revolutionaries, I guess.

For many nights, while hearing the pounding on the door—the ugliest noise ever made by men—we sat quietly among books written by the most beautiful minds of the world: great books by Li Bai, Confucius, Lao Tzu, Chang Tzu, Einstein, and Shakespeare. We took great risks in order to protect those books. House searches stopped in a few weeks, but the Cultural Revolution was to continue for 10 more years, with schools closed and most books banned. Fortunately, our books remained, and we remained connected to the world. My family defeated the Cultural Revolution in an isolated battle. During China's darkest years, I found comfort and inspiration among those books of science, literature, and history. They were my solid ground for connections.

Even today, I like to stay among books and journals in a library, reading, researching, and writing as if behind the Great Wall: safe against the sound and fury of the world. Sometimes I just sit quietly with a book on my lap, trying to connect myself to the mysterious universe or looking through the window to the horizon, as if there is something between the sky and the earth. (I call it thinking, but my wife calls it wasting time). I like to sit in a sanctuary of learning, where mellow silence reigns and I do not hear the piercing pounding on the door.

But I would like to warn you today, especially after the events of September 11: Please do not take your sense of safety for granted. No culture is immune to disasters. If you allow yourselves to be disconnected from the world, you may hear that ugly knocking at your door.

Appendix B

In Memory of Hai Zi, Who Died for Beauty

Hai Zi (1964–1989) was an ephemeral star among the "obscure poets" that emerged after China's 1979 reforms. He dazzled the world twice: the first time when he was accepted by the prestigious Beijing University at the age of 15, the second time when he committed suicide by laying himself on a railway track at the age of 25. Between these two events, he left a bright trail that is composed of 2 million characters of poetry and prose.

Hai Zi was not my friend when he was alive, but he is now in his death. According to *About the Death of Hai Zi* by his best friend Xi Chuan, Hai Zi carried four books to the railway tracks: the Bible, Thoreau's *Walden*, Thor Heyerdahl's *Kon-Tiki: Across the Pacific by Raft*, and *Selected Novels of Joseph Conrad*. I was saddened and flattered when I saw the title of the last book that Hai Zi took to another world, because I compiled, cotranslated, and prefaced the *Selected Novels of Joseph Conrad*. Before leaving for the United States in 1982, I handed the manuscript to the publisher, and I had scarcely heard anything about it after that. Now I received the most overwhelming feedback that an author or translator can hope for. Hai Zi is no stranger anymore. I did not know I had such a sincere friend and fellow traveler. Together we penetrated the heart of darkness and sailed through a typhoon. We went there together. We both decided we liked the beauty in those places. I left, but he stayed there forever.

Hai Zi died in the line of beauty just as some martyrs die in the line of duty. Beauty's way of treating us is different from duty's way. Ellen Sturgis Hooper's (1816–1841) poem discusses the relationship between duty and beauty:

> I slept, and dreamed that life was Beauty;
> I woke, and found that life was Duty.
> Was thy dream then a shadowy lie?
> Toil on, poor heart, unceasingly;
> And thou shalt find thy dream to be
> A truth and noonday light to thee.

Duty commands, beauty inspires. Beauty is freedom; duty is constraint. Yet our relationship to beauty is the same as our relationship to duty. We can reject beauty's appeal, as we can reject duty's command; yet duty, like beauty, cannot be rebuffed with impunity. Hai Zi rebuffed duty in the name of beauty. He paid for beauty with the dearest price—his life.

Hai Zi is a quixotic hero. He began by testing his mind against the world and ended by destroying his body for spiritual freedom. He believed that he could shape Chinese reality into the foreign images of the Messiah's paradise, Thoreau's Walden Pond, Heyerdahl's raft, and Conrad's ocean. Like Don Quixote, he was doomed to fail heroically. This Chinese knight-errant broke himself against the bars of his self-built prison. He belongs to no world, neither foreign nor Chinese. He focused too much on his spiritual odyssey without preparation of his sailing skills. He loved the ocean, but he could not swim. He loved romance, but he could not dance. He loved the earth, but he could not ride a bike. He loved life, but he could not live. He loved beauty, and he succeeded in creating a unique and original world of words and rhythms. In that sense, he is triumphant.

Hai Zi must have read the following epitaph inscribed on Conrad's gravestone at St. Thomas Church, Canterbury, England. I translated and quoted it in the preface of *Selected Novels of Joseph Conrad*:

> Sleep after toyle, port after stormie seas,
> Ease after warre, death after life, does greatly please.

I believe this poem by George John Spencer did not cause Hai Zi's death but confirmed his desire to find rest in eternity. He chose to die for beauty, just as some people choose to die for truth. Hai Zi's epitaph should be Emily Dickinson's poem:

> I died for beauty but was scarce
> Adjusted in the tomb,
> When one who died for truth was lain
> In an adjoining room.
> He questioned softly why I failed?
> "For beauty," I replied.
> "And I for truth—the two are one;
> We brethren are," he said.
> And so, as kinsmen met a-night,

We talked between the rooms,
Until the moss had reached our lips,
And covered up our names.

Or Tao Yuanming's, "Lament":

What you can say about death
Just identify the body with the mountains

Or, more properly, Hai Zi's own poem; "Spring, Ten Hai Zi":

Spring. Ten Hai Zi all resurrected.
In the bright scene
They mock at this one barbaric and sad Hai Zi
Why on earth do you sleep such a dead, long sleep?
Spring. Ten Hai Zi rage and roar under breath
They dance and sing around you and me
Tear disheveled your black hair, ride on you and fly away,
stirring up a cloud of dust
Your pain of being cleaved open pervades the great earth
In the spring, barbaric and grief-stricken Hai Zi
Only this one is left, the last one
A child of dark night, immersed in winter, addicted to death
He cannot help himself, and loves the empty and cold village
There crops piled high up, covering up the window
They use half of the corn to feed the six mouths of the family,
eating and stomach
The other half was used in agriculture, their own procreation
Strong wind sweeps from the east to the west, from the north to the
south, blind to dark night and dawn

What on earth is the meaning of dawn that you spoke of?[12]

Hai Zi did what he said and killed himself near the starting point of the Great Wall, where the mountains meet the ocean. His death was a gallant and romantic declaration of his passions, devotions, and beliefs. People finally believed he meant what he had "roared" in his poems, when he willingly returned to the mountains and ocean.

Poetry hides behind the opening and closing of a door, leaving those who look through to guess about what could be seen when the door was open. Hai Zi's poems, like the marks left in the snow by goose tracks, are the traces of his life. Now, let us open the door and let our ephemeral star be seen.

NOTES

11. Hai Zi, *An English Translation of Poems of the Contemporary Chinese Poet Hai Zi*, trans. Hong Zeng (Lewiston, New York: Edwin Mellen Press, 2006).

Appendix C
Student Contributions

In a recent class, 59 students of Carleton College, all members of Qiguang Zhao's course, The Taoist Way of Health and Longevity: Tai Chi and Other Forms, were divided into six groups and wrote their own manifestos of Applied New Taoism.

Students were also asked to keep a journal of their reactions to the class lectures. The included excerpts from group manifestos and class journals are the products of ten weeks of reflection on both Taoist philosophy and how to apply that philosophy to modern life. The following are their words, either as a group or as individuals.

Student Groups:

Ganbei:
Caitlin Bowersox
David Chin
Rachel Danner
Lianne Hilbert
Craig Hogle
Karen Lee
Matthew Shelton

Like Water:
Naomi Hattori
Aaron Kaufman
Marie Kim
Paul Koenig
Nora Mahlberg
Nelupa Perera
Charles Yi

Old Fishermen:

William Bennett
Philip Casken
Anna Ing
David Kamin
Sophie Kerman
Greg Marliave
Carisa Skretch
Andrew Ullman

The Sorting:

Alex Baum
Jean Hyun
YoonJung Ku
He Sun
Chris Young
Xiuyuan Geoffrey Yu

The Place Where the Water Meets the Sand:

Becky Alexander
Matt Bartel
Elizabeth Graff
Mark Stewart
Aaron Weiner
Kristi Welle
Katie Whillock

The Sound of One Hand Clapping:

Jacob Hitchcock
Anthony McElligott
Lauren Milne
Megan Molteni
Emily Muirhead
Peter Olds
Sam Rober

The concept of Wu Wei is illustrated by the tale of two men stranded in rapids. The first, being too old and weak to fight the current, lets it carry him downstream. By surrendering to the current, he is swept out to calm waters. The second man tries to fight the current and drowns. The old man discovered the nature of water, became water, and was brought to safety. You cannot fight nature; it is arrogant to think that you can change the path of the eternal.

—*The Sound of One Hand Clapping*

By attempting to "return to the source," we are trying to attain a higher state of thinking, a state of nothingness. It is not a state that implies ignorance or pessimism, but a state that rejects attempts to regulate society or go against the natural flow.

—*Ganbei*

Not every problem needs fixing, and not everything that looks wrong is broken.

—*Alex Baum*

We are like a drop of water in a river. We do not notice that we are moving, because the rest of the water drops are also moving. We strive to move ourselves when all we really need to do is rest and move with the flow of the universe.

—*Dan Edwards*

We are on a rambling path; we should pay attention to the present. There should be a balance between understanding that we are part of a whole, stretching across time and space, and realizing that we are limited in some regard to our time and space. To ignore this is to ignore where our rambling path has taken us.

I consider it like a great mural: for example, the Sistine Chapel. Certainly Michelangelo had a sense of the work as a whole, but at the same time, each individual part needed special care and attention in order for the whole to succeed.

—*Greg Marliave*

It's a marvelous moment when you see a constellation clearly, or see a tree in bloom in the spring, but it also makes you think, "Why didn't I notice it earlier?"

—*Jenny Oyallon-Koloski*

The most stunning aspects of the universe are effortless—the planets, moons, and stars move with majestic ease. The beauty of the water flowing, birds flying, and trees waving in the wind all occur without effort.

—*Mark Severtsgaard*

Through Taoism, I have realized that my role in the universe is not one of great importance. In so doing, I become a part of the universe and a master of the universe as well. I do not understand the universe yet, because I do not know myself fully, but the goal is not the destination. The goal to know myself lies in the journey, for in the journey lie beauty and knowledge.

—*The Sound of One Hand Clapping*

I've noticed in my travels that in places where there is a lot of space (the great outdoors or small towns), time seems to slow down and stop at times, but when space is limited (in a big city) time stops for no man.

—*Kristi Welle*

We are now unable to instinctively understand [Taoist] concepts, for our minds have been crowded with material-istic worries. Taoism is not looking to transform us into a brand new being; rather, it seeks to return the being back to its original state at the beginning of time, away from the corruption that society has instilled upon humans. In this state, one will be yielding, free, and effortless.

—*Karen Lee*

Everything needs its opposite to exist. Without an opposite, you cannot define yourself.

—*Peter Olds*

The moon leads, and the tides follow.
For what does the moon care for the tides?
The tree grows and sprouts new leaves.
But what do the roots know of blooming?

Erase distinction and the roots feed the leaves,
The tides move with the moon.

The sages see good in simplicity:
The ocean at war with the moon, who would think it?
In ebbing and flowing as one, they feed us all.
If the roots forgot the tree, both would die.

—*Old Fishermen*

To illustrate the principle of reversal, let us consider the motion of water. First, we have waves. Waves flow toward the shore, but when they arrive there, they recede. Second, and on a grander scale, we have the tides. Over a period of hours, the water on a beach will move up the shore until it reaches the high tide point, and then it reverses. When we consider that the tides are caused by the moon, it seems almost certain that reversal is a cosmic principle.

The principle of reversal is also evident in our daily lives. When we realize that we have made a mistake, we correct that mistake by changing our actions to the opposite of what we had been doing. That is, we must reverse. The principle of reversal also plays out over the course of our lives. We are born completely dependent upon others for our survival. As time passes, our demands on others lessen until we reach independence. However, as we continue to age, we become dependent upon others for more and more until we cannot survive without them.

—Like Water

When we discussed reversing today, I was reminded of the first art class I ever took. For the first six weeks of class, we weren't allowed to use erasers when we drew. Our teacher told us that this exercise would teach us how to trust our instincts. More often than not, the first line you draw is better than any other you draw in its place. Whenever I erase over and over again, I usually just end up either starting over or coming back to the original line! It seems it is better to trust your instincts than to keep drawing and drawing, only to end up back at the same place you started.

—Marie Kim

The sage makes cryptic remarks,
He speaks in generalities.
By naming one thing,
He names all of the ten thousand things.
By naming nothing,
He names that which escapes all words.
He calls it Tao.
When speaking of it, he does not define it.
When asked to define it, he does not speak.

—Old Fishermen

If I name something, I am separating it from other things. But the Tao is not separable; one cannot take a knife to the universe and cut out a slice that is Tao. In the words of Bruce Lee, "It is like a finger pointing at the moon. Do not look at the finger, or you will miss all of that heavenly glory." Here, language is our finger. Lao Tzu is pointing at the Tao, but if one looks too hard at the words, one misses the point entirely.

—Will Bennett

When thinking about naming things, I think about Shakespeare: "What's in a name? That which we call a rose by any other name would smell as sweet." People get wrapped up in names: when a mother is with child, the first question is, "Have you thought of names?" When something new is created, we wonder what to call it, but in the end, it doesn't matter.

—Kristi Welle

Perhaps the idea of an empty vessel is an encouragement not to save anything for later. Do not save your cute underwear for a special day; make today your special day.

—Becky Alexander

To someone living in the wealthiest nation in the world, it has been difficult to come to terms with the idea of not filling to the brim. We live in a world of "all-you-can-eat-for-$6.95," far from the concept that fully stretching oneself is actually detrimental to one's health and state of mind.

—Megan Molteni

We live in a consumer economy that, through regular and repeated advertising, leads us to believe that the only way to achieve happiness is through money and material possessions. We live in a world where we must super-size to get our money's worth. If we look toward modern culture in order to find happiness, we will most likely find ourselves feeling unfulfilled. No matter how much we try to fill our lives to the brim, we still long for something more.

Instead, look inward. Just as the Tao is an empty vessel, we must look to rid ourselves of our dependence on material objects. It is not our possessions that determine our worth. True usefulness does not come from the container that is filled to the brim but the container that is empty. Only when we are empty can we put our own materials in, not what others tell us we should have.

—Ganbei

The water carries the boat.
If the fisherman is restless, the boat will tip.
If he does nothing, he will forever drift.
But if he guides his boat with the current,
He will find what he seeks.

—Old Fishermen

What there is now is all that there is.
Thoughts of what was, or what could be,
Bring nothing but worry and remorse.
If we rid our mind of what is not,
We are left only with happiness of what is.

—Old Fishermen

Is escape always good? Shouldn't we face the trials of life rather than running from them? Doing nothing isn't the same as avoiding everything.

—Sophie Kerman

Riding the tides of nocturnal oblivion, one can reflect upon the Tao. Only in sleep can this truly happen, because one cannot coherently think; one can only be guided by the cycles of the mind. Only when you release all aspirations, all goals, all feelings of being, when through living you come closest to death, can one meet the Tao.

—The Sorting

None of us knows if we are ourselves. I cannot tell, when I close my eyes at night, if the world exists while I am sleeping. Each of us may be a butterfly dreaming—reversing each night as we go to sleep.

—The Place Where the Water Meets the Sand

If we cannot tell what is real and what isn't, we may as well make beauty where we can, and hope the ugliness is part of the illusion.

—*Sophie Kerman*

We fill our bellies with breaths so that we can empty our hearts of thought. In breathing with our whole bodies and seeing beyond the fragmentation of our own bodies, we may begin to see beyond the superficial fragmentation of the universe.

—*The Place Where the Water Meets the Sand*

I've written 20-page papers and solved complex mathematical problems. But to return to my roots, to completely relearn how to do something I've known since birth, to relearn how to breathe was the most complicated obstacle by far.

—*Karen Lee*

If you ignore your own ignorance, you will be unable to further your learning. You will remain ignorant and will only think you know all.

—*Anthony McElligott*

The eventual understanding of your own spirit is the greatest pursuit of knowledge we can and should be engaged in. Scholastic learning may seem impressive, but when compared to enlightenment, it is nothing.

—*Aaron Kaufman*

You have to learn something in order to unlearn it. Is that what Lao Tzu means, that the goal isn't learning but rather unlearning?

—*Sophie Kerman*

Do you not have to learn Taoism? Can you not learn from the world? How can you change if you do not learn? Humans seem to have to learn everything—it's part of our nature; that's how we grow. How can we refuse our nature?

—*Lauren Milne*

I wonder if this alludes less to the meaning of learning and more to our concept of worry. Worry is a learned reaction. Could Lao Tzu mean to say, "Forget how you learned about worry, for I wish to teach you a new way to process the events that would have caused you worry?"

—*Kristi Welle*

We need to return to our roots: eat when we're hungry, sleep when we're tired, scratch where it itches, without rudeness or reservations.

—*Becky Alexander*

Taoists *do* do everything backwards. Everyone else cannot wait to grow up. Taoists say no; we will return to infancy. We will feed our bellies and not worry about the tiny trials in our own lives. We will be the blank slate.

—*Megan Molteni*

The Taoist path is rambling,
The path cannot be planned.
Dwell in the future or the past,
And you will never be prepared.
Go forward with no presumptions about the future,
And you will always be prepared.
Remember that the present happens only once,
Do not waste your opportunity.
The future will always be on the horizon,
Do not let it distract you from the present.

—*Greg Marliave*

What do we do with real and immediate conflict? We can
carry the Tao internally, but when someone faces us with an
egregious wrongdoing, what do we do, from a Taoist stand-
point? Should we let people be killed, because there are no
distinctions between wrong and right? Because they'll just
die later anyway?

—*Sophie Kerman*

A rose is not pretty to become pretty, but its design for itself
makes it beautiful.

—*Gregory Ely*

Life is about expression and passion. Without the two you
cannot live. You may live, but unperceived by others, unac-
knowledged by the future. This is like life without life, an
eternal death. We can do nothing about death, but we can
make life the true opposite of death through expression.

—*Peter Olds*

In music, the beauty comes from both the notes and the spaces between the notes. The opposites are united, and in synthesis form something greater than themselves.

—*Andrew Ullman*

I think the best art captures a moment of universality, one moment that is made eternal. Why would we need to immortalize the look in one person's eyes, or the fall of a leaf from a tree, if these things weren't constantly escaping us?

Could we say that art reverses the deteriorating process of time? Yet at the same time, art ages and deteriorates, and its meaning always changes, even to the same person (who is different the next time they see it). Art encapsulates both life and death.

—*Sophie Kerman*

We are completely dependent on the universe. But in that dependency we find the freedom not to worry.

—*Sophie Kerman*

Life and death are not interchangeable for those whom we care for. Even if time is not well defined, I still have to live my life with someone I care about. That alone is worth ensuring that we value life.

—*Craig Hogle*

Sometimes we need to stop being cosmic, come back down to earth, and realize that we are all human, and we all need some simple human pleasures: music, love, friendship, playfulness, good food, dancing, whatever you like.

—*Mark Stewart*

If we are not trying to win, we cannot lose, and thus, there is never an outcome unless there is one of "winning."

—*Mark Stewart*

Be spontaneous
Go where the winds will take you
The Tao will find you

Let the quick fox jump
I will be the lazy dog
Yet achieve my goal
Leave time in your day
The work you do is valued
The peace is priceless

—*Becky Alexander*

Is it better to do great things with knowledge and ability, or to lead a simple life without ambition? Is there a way to lead a "great" and Taoist life?

—*Matt Bartel*

There is no purpose in life. We have made ourselves a purpose, because we cannot deal with life without it.

—*Caitlin Bowersox*

I am who I am: who are you?

—*Rachel Danner*

What makes us more special than a pine tree? At least the pine is content with itself and does not envy the flowers growing nearby. At least the pine does its job its whole life, without whining and complaining. Humans are flawed in so many ways that we are unaware of.

—*Calvin Lieu*

As we move into the future, we create technological innovations at increasing rates. We are like the man with the great wagon, the great horse, and the great driver. Now, our wagon is even better; it is a jet plane. We have made the horse obsolete, for it is too slow. Our pilots are better; they attend flight school for years. However, it is of no use to have these things if we move in the wrong direction. As we continue to get higher and faster, we must not forget the lessons that can be learned from going slower, lower, and weaker.

—*Old Fishermen*

If you have any goals, you are not free to renounce things.

—*The Sorting*

Taoism sometimes makes me think of the Robert Frost poem, "The Road Not Taken." Most people think that Frost was glad he took the road less traveled by, but that's not what he said. He said that it made all the difference. Who knows what that difference was? I suppose Taoism would have me take the path that leads downhill. But if you always go downhill, you'll never get to see the sunrise over the trees.

—*Matt Bartel*

If we did not have an end to strive for, would we even bother taking the journey? I'd like to think we would, but I'm a bit doubtful.

—*Jenny Oyallon-Koloski*

Tai Chi under the stars is very calming. In one way it is like being left alone in the world. When no one else is awake or outside, you can truly be alone. On the other hand, everything that is not out during the day comes out during the night, so you can connect with the other half of the world.

—Emily Muirhead

"You don't need a badge on your sleeve to have honor." *—A Few Good Men*

—Becky Alexander

Hatred and rancor are poisonous. Times I've been filled with them—and they've been few, thank God—I've ended up literally feeling physically ill! If that's not evidence, I don't know what is.

—Paul Koenig

One who practices moral conduct will share the happiness of others and experience the pain of those who are suffering. They will be humble and not envy or act in anger. By following moral conduct, they will help maintain the rhythm of nature, which in turn leads them to the way of the universe.

—Nelupa Perera

When we are kind to people and greet everyone we meet with positive, free flowing energy, with smiles, we are creating a new kind of uniform motion! Perhaps warmth will flow from one person to the next. Nothing will be lost, and everyone will gain.

—Eleni Schirmer

If you own nothing, you will lose nothing.
If you desire nothing, you will never be left wanting.
The pain of loss is self-inflicted.
The joy of contentedness is self-protecting.
Accept what is now as perfect
And you will never be unhappy.

—Old Fishermen

My birth was not my beginning, because I am unborn, and
my death will not be my end, because I am ever-living.

—Andrew Ullman

One can love both life and death. Not being afraid of death
doesn't mean one can't work to prolong life.

—Alex Baum

If someone wants to party all night long, it doesn't
necessarily mean they're afraid of going to bed.

—Jessica Taylor

We don't cry for people when they die; we cry for ourselves
because we are alone.

—Caitlin Bowersox

If we always fear death, then we can never enjoy life. People
who live in fear of death will rarely do anything that may
pose a risk. Rather than fearing the end, we should think in
the reverse and take comfort in the fact that we are aware of
our limited time on earth. With this knowledge, we can try
to live every moment to the fullest.

—Naomi Hattori

Why do we fear the unknown? Is the known always worth holding onto?

—Paul Koenig

In modern life, we try to physically ward off death by quitting smoking or wearing a seatbelt. We are always fighting someone outside of ourselves. In Taoism, the true enemy is one's traditional mindset. When Zhuangzi's wife died, he played the drums. He defeated death not through action, but through a change in perspective.

—Lauren Milne

Really being accepting of death and suffering at any moment means one must be content with life.

—Kristi Welle

About the Author

Qiguang Zhao is Burton and Lily Levin Professor of Chinese at Carleton College, Northfield, Minnesota. He was born in Beijing and grew up in China. He has an MA in English and American literature from the Chinese Academy of Social Sciences and a Ph.D. in Comparative Literature from the University of Massachusetts, Amherst.

He started the Chinese Language program at Carleton College and has been teaching courses in Chinese language and literature, comparative literature, and Taoism for 20 years. He leads a study-abroad program in China every other year. His teaching method, *huajiang,* supplements lecture with the lively cartoons that he draws on the board. His favorite course, The Taoist Way of Health and Longevity: Tai Chi and Other Forms, is one of the most popular courses at Carleton College. It has moved to larger and larger classrooms from term to term. In this course, students learn how Taoism and Tai Chi can improve the quality of modern life.

Qiguang Zhao has frequently appeared on Chinese television, discussing culture and international relations. Recently, he talked about Taoism on Shanghai television in a ten-part series called "The Wisdom of Lao Tzu," which was broadcast in November 2007 and will be published in book form. He has also judged the International Emmy Awards. He has published six books, including a comparative study of Eastern and Western dragons.

Qiguang Zhao in front of a statue of Lao Tzu of Song Dynasty, Fujian Province, China.

Students of Carleton College and Qiguang Zhao perform Tai Chi on the Great Wall, 2006.

Qiguang Zhao and Students in the class of Taoist Way of Health and Longevity, Carleton College, 2008.

Bibliography

Birch, Cyril, ed. *Anthology of Chinese Literature*. New York: Grove Press, 1965.

Chen, Ellen. *The Tao Te Ching: A New Translation with Commentary*. St. Paul, MN: Paragon House, 1989.

Chen Yaoting, ed. *Daojia Yangshengshu* (Taoist Way of Health and Longevity). Shanghai: Fudan University Press, 1992.

Confucius. *The Analects*. Arthur Waley, trans. Hertfordshire: Wordsworth Editions Limited, 1996.

Hawking, Stephen. *The Theory of Everything*. Beverly Hills: New Millennium Press, 2002.

Lao Tsu. *Tao Te Ching*. Gia-Fu Feng and Jane English, trans. New York: Vintage Books, 1989.

Liezi. *Liezi*. Liang Xiaopeng and Li Jianguo, trans. Beijing: Zhonghua Book Company, 2005.

Tagore, Rabindranath. *Stray Birds*. Old Chelsea Station, NY: Cosimo Classics, 2004.

Zhuangzi. *The Inner Chapters*. A.C. Graham, trans. Indianapolis: Hackett Publishing Company, Inc., 2001.

Index

Liu Zongyuan 111, 112
longevity 26, 69, 70, 71, 75, 169,
    177, 199, 203
Lord Byron 162
love 4, 38, 81, 89, 107, 111, 113,
    115, 117, 122, 129, 133,
    134, 135, 136, 137, 142,
    143, 185, 204, 215, 216,
    231, 235

M

Mark Twain 70, 78
Marx 104
Master Lai 126, 128
Master Li 126, 128
Master Si 126, 127
Master Yu 126
Mencius 6, 84
mind 2, 3, 12, 21, 60, 63, 65, 66,
    72, 79, 83, 84, 86, 95, 97,
    98, 99, 104, 105, 108, 121,
    124, 128, 131, 133, 150,
    155, 157, 158, 163, 165,
    166, 167, 169, 171, 173,
    178, 179, 181, 183, 186,
    192, 194, 195, 212, 214,
    223, 224, 226, 227, 236
Ming Dynasty 157
Mona Lisa 131
moon 15, 56, 81, 124, 129, 143,
    165, 173, 188, 189, 190,
    191, 210, 222, 223, 224,
    225
mountain 12, 13, 23, 30, 64, 70,
    72, 84, 108, 129, 130, 143,
    168, 177, 188, 190, 195,

    204, 216, 217
movement 36, 43, 44, 64, 83, 95,
    141, 165, 168, 169, 171,
    172, 173, 174, 177, 179,
    183, 193
mystery 54, 186

N

name 1, 12, 22, 27, 49, 50, 52,
    106, 111, 122, 125, 137,
    147, 158, 173, 214, 216,
    225
nature 1, 2, 11, 19, 22, 24, 29, 32,
    38, 39, 47, 52, 53, 59, 60,
    65, 66, 96, 101, 103, 105,
    122, 124, 125, 126, 128,
    131, 134, 140, 141, 142,
    143, 144, 145, 163, 172,
    187, 190, 209, 221, 229,
    234
Nature 38, 64, 66, 129, 131, 143,
    175, 179, 189, 204
Newton 171
nonaction 1, 12, 19, 20, 22, 26,
    29, 31, 53, 60, 63, 79, 87,
    99, 100, 101, 136, 157

P

peace 23, 24, 25, 58, 59, 97, 162,
    165, 167, 174, 177, 194,
    195, 203, 232
Peace 24
Peking Opera 7, 81
people 5, 6, 12, 16, 23, 26, 36,
    38, 45, 56, 57, 63, 66, 71,
    72, 73, 74, 78, 79, 80, 83,